WORN STORIES

WORN STORIES

EMILY SPIVACK

PRINCETON ARCHITECTURAL PRESS

NEW YORK

it gives me a great pleasure to keep my clo
thes my dresses, my stockings, I have never thrown away a pair
of shoes of mine in 20 years. I cannot separate
myself from my clothes nor Alain's – The pretext
is that they are still good – it is my past and as
rotten *as it was I would like to take it and*
hold it tight in my arms

—LOUISE BOURGEOIS, 1968

INTRODUCTION

On a brisk winter day in late 2013, I took my students on a tour of a national thrift-store chain's largest distribution center in Brooklyn as part of an undergraduate course I was teaching. The four-story building—a converted horse stable built in the early 1800s—was humming with activity. We were shown each floor's dedicated purpose in sifting through the tons of clothing, as well as bric-a-brac, electronics, and furniture, that arrive each day. Jeans, T-shirts, skirts, unworn designer wedding dresses, shoes, winter coats, and bathing suits were emptied by the truckload each morning on the first floor. Then they were sorted, priced, and hung on plastic hangers on the third floor, brought to the store on the second floor, put into out-of-season storage on the fourth floor, or taken back down to the first floor, where they were reloaded onto a truck and taken to another one of the thrift store's many locations throughout Brooklyn.

The sheer quantity of clothing passing through this facility—about ten thousand pieces per day—was astounding. Even more eye-opening was what happened to the clothes that weren't deemed worthy by the store's sorters. They were dumped down a chute, called "the hole." The mounds of clothes landed in a bin on the first floor and piled up until a machine compressed them into thousand-pound cubes. Those packages were then sold in bulk to distributors who shipped them to third-world countries or shredded them into rags.

The clothes were no longer recognizable for their function or style after they had been packed into cubes. It was hard to believe that someone had once worn them. You know when you repeat a word over and over, and suddenly the word becomes unfamiliar, strange-sounding? It was like that, but with clothes. They became meaningless stuff. Each garment had lost all attachment to its previous owner and its intended use. It had nothing to do with fashion. And there was just so much of it.

Who had worn the garment before it was donated to the thrift store? Where had it been? What was the previous owner like? Except for a lingering scent of perfume or body odor, a stain, or a movie stub in the pocket of a pair of jeans, that history, and each garment's provenance, was lost.

These are questions I was asking when I started the *Worn Stories* project in 2010. I was curious about our garments' histories and wanted to create a place to record and preserve these stories: first, my own; then, entries from my friends and family; and, eventually, the stories of strangers.

Our clothes are full of memory and meaning. That's why we all have garments—hanging in our closets, shoved in the backs of drawers, and boxed up in garages—that we haven't worn in years but just can't part with. And then there are the clothes we wear every day, whose stories are still unfolding.

My own closet is full of clothes; it is also an evolving archive of experiences, adventures, and memories. I began using my clothes to write about those experiences—my first concert T-shirt, a hand-me-down scarf, a handmade sweater. Quickly, three things became clear: First, clothes can be a rich and universal storytelling device. Second, I was much more interested in the clothing-inspired narratives of other people than in my own. And third, if those stories aren't captured, they disappear.

For the *Worn Stories* website, wornstories.com, and eventually for this book, I asked for stories from people I knew or admired—artists, musicians, writers, filmmakers, chefs, entrepreneurs, and designers. I put out a call to friends and acquaintances I'd known for years. And I solicited contributions on the *Worn Stories* website, from listservs, and via Craigslist. Most contributors told me their stories; others wrote them themselves. In each case, the request was the same: Select a piece of clothing still in your possession with a compelling story behind it, whether something

spectacular, unexpected, weird, wonderful, or momentous happened while you were wearing it. And share what you remember. As a result, the subject matter of these tales ranges from the everyday to the extraordinary. They include recollections about clothing worn during a breakup and during a kidnapping, while accidentally tripping on acid and while taking aerobics classes, on a visit to the White House and on a trek along the Great Wall of China.

The intent of this book is simple: that these tales will not only offer a glimpse into the lives of these contributors but also prompt you, the reader, to reconsider the role of clothing in your own life—before your clothes someday wind up in anonymous piles like those I saw at the thrift store's distribution facility.

The clothes that protect us, that make us laugh, that serve as a uniform, that help us assert our identity or aspirations, that we wear to remember someone—in all of these are encoded the stories of our lives. We all have a memoir in miniature living in a garment we've worn. This book brings some of those stories to light.

—EMILY SPIVACK

Andy Spade

My job is to give this jacket a second life. The woman who sold it to me at a flea market on 25th Street told me it had been sitting in her attic for fifteen years, since her husband died. When I got it, it was barely wearable because it was so stiff, and it was covered in dust. Anytime I would wear it, I'd come home and my wife, Kate, would say, "Your shirt and pants have green dust on them." It bleeds whenever I wear it. I'm not being a weirdo, but I feel like I have a part of this person on me, like I'm actually borrowing his character.

I did an ad campaign for a clothing company that makes chinos. The tagline for the campaign was "You can't get them old until you get them new." I hate when designers make things look fake old—with splatter paint or acid wash, for example. With this coat, it's already old, and I want to take care of it, for the guy who had it before me.

When I started my clothing and accessories company, I said to my wife, "The only thing that's missing is a hundred years of history. I guess I have to start now." In a hundred years someone will carry one of my bags and it will mean something. Today it doesn't, but as it's lived in, it will.

Not only does this jacket's history leave its residue on me—and I don't mind the dirt—it's also musty, because it was in the attic for so many years. That mustiness is better than any perfume. I don't wear perfume. I prefer wearing jackets that smell like they've had lives. That's my cologne—a dirty, musty jacket.

—AS TOLD TO EMILY SPIVACK

Andy Spade is the cofounder of Partners & Spade
and Sleepy Jones.

Simon Doonan

One by one my roommates, friends, and boyfriends in Los Angeles started getting sick from AIDS. It was very early on in the epidemic and when you went to the doctor, they couldn't refer you to an expert. They asked you if you were religious, meaning, you were going to die.

I decided to join a gym with a friend who had been diagnosed with AIDS. At least we could be healthy, we thought. We became members of Sports Connection, also known as "Sports Erection," in West Hollywood. This was in the early 1980s during the aerobics heyday in Los Angeles, when Jane Fonda had her own aerobics studio and women walked around in pastel blue Lycra tights with pink leg warmers, white Reeboks, and sweatbands.

Going to aerobics became an obsession. I have a low center of gravity and very strong legs, so I was instantly very good at following all the routines. I'd power through an hour of exercise and sweat a lot—so as not to get squat. My mother used to say to my sister and me, "Now you're both short; you don't want to become squat." She always wore long-line girdles and smoked cigarettes so she wouldn't get fat. I had aerobics.

I was working at Maxfield back then, which was the first groovy designer shop in L.A. Customers like Fleetwood Mac, Natalie Wood, Cher, Linda Ronstadt, and Joni Mitchell would shop there because it was the first place in L.A. where you could buy Alaïa, Comme des Garçons, or Versace. They also carried Stephen Sprouse. He did these Lycra cycle pant things for men that were orange and black with mirror graffiti writing on them, and I thought they would be great for aerobics. When I look at them now, I hear the disco version of *Cats*, lots of Pointer Sisters, and all the aerobics anthems that were so popular back then.

I went every day. In an attempt to do "healthy" things, I became addicted to the lights, the music, the endorphins. It was a very showbiz-y way to keep in shape, and many actresses would go to the class, like Madonna when she was starting to become well known. They filmed the aerobics movie *Perfect*, with John Travolta and Jamie Lee Curtis, at Sports Connection about six months after we joined. Curtis had the ultimate aerobics body—legs, legs, legs, and very toned arms.

All that exhibitionism appealed to me. I always threw on my Lycra, strode into class, stood right in front of the mirror, and got into it. And I was the only one wearing these super New Wave, groovy Lycra leggings.

At the time, I was very into the New Romantic look. I had a lot of that Vivienne Westwood pirate clothing, and I'm in the "Bette Davis Eyes" video, by Kim Carnes. That look was big in L.A. and London. What's noteworthy is that back then I could go out with my New Romantic friends in the evening and chuck on my leggings for aerobics the next day. There wasn't this slavish desire to be cool. It wasn't about sucking in your cheeks or money or table service or prestige. It was more about having fun, being fun, being stupid, being mad, being theatrical, being as naff as you wanted.

English people are acutely aware of what's naff and what's not, but we willfully embrace naff things. I knew that doing aerobics was one of the naffest things I could do, but I loved it because I was in charge of my own naffness.

The cult of aerobics was waning by the time I moved to New York in 1985, but with so many people getting sick, for a couple of years it was an antidote to this incredible malaise of melancholy that had been blanketing L.A.

—AS TOLD TO EMILY SPIVACK

Simon Doonan is the creative ambassador-at-large of the New York City–based clothing store Barneys. He is also the author of *Beautiful People* and *The Asylum*.

Greta Gerwig

Twelve years ago I was working as a stage manager at a theater company in Vermont for the summer. I was the worst stage manager of all time.

Around this time, I figured out that I could fall in love with people and that I could be in love. I was already in love with one person, and I started falling in love with lots of people. I felt very guilty about it, but it also felt like an appropriate response to figuring out you can be in love. I was in love with love. In high school I would have these horrible crushes on people but they were never reciprocated or the people were gay. Then, in college, I had the experience of looking into someone's eyes and saying, "I love you" and he said, "I love you" back.

I had this crush, or love, for this actor at the theater in Vermont. His name was David, and I thought he was so beautiful. He had this very soft button-down shirt. When I hugged him, and I would always invent reasons to do so, I would touch his shirt. It was very chaste, and nothing ever happened. I was in love with him, but he was twenty-six-years old and I was eighteen, and when you're eighteen, twenty-six seems really old.

David left that summer before I did. We took him to the bus station, and I cried because I was eighteen and dramatic. I watched him go and I felt bereft. My friends and I returned to the falling-apart cabin in the woods that had been our home that summer. I went to the room where I had a bunk bed. Hanging on my bunk was that button-down shirt, his shirt! Tucked inside the shirt pocket was a note. He told me I was beautiful and a creature of light.

Doesn't it just kill you? Can you imagine an eighteen-year-old girl coming back from the bus station to her room and seeing that the guy she loved had left his shirt for her? He knew. He just knew it, and it was beautiful.

I always write in the shirt because it makes me feel like I have a secret. When you write, it's good to have a secret because in a way you do. You have to nurture the secret until other people know about it. Maybe wearing this shirt connects me with a part of my younger self that was incredibly emotional and vivid, and those feelings, combined with that sense of having a secret, is how I like to feel when I write.

—AS TOLD TO EMILY SPIVACK

Greta Gerwig is an actress and filmmaker known for her roles in *Frances Ha*, *Greenberg*, and *Damsels in Distress*.

Ross Intelisano

My grandmother, Anna Leonardi Intelisano, emigrated from Sicily to Queens, New York, in 1946 because war-torn Italy provided little opportunity for work. She left behind a baby (my father), a husband, and a huge extended family. Anna cleaned houses and then became a seamstress. She saved enough cash to bring my grandfather and father to the U.S., and her sister and brother, too. For many years, Anna left her house before dawn to open the seamstress shop where she worked. She eventually rose to the rank of sample dressmaker for Diane von Furstenberg and Maggie London. She spoke an eclectic mix of Sicilian dialect, Italian, and broken English. She was a master cook of lasagna, cutlets, and marinara sauce. Anna took care of everyone.

In her "spare" time, Anna created vibrant dresses, scarves, and ties. My father always wore her ties. If anyone ever complimented one of them, my father would simply take it off and give it away. I've seen him do it a hundred times, even to strangers.

My immigrant father hustled his way to middle-class life, and in 1975, when I was six, we moved to a house right on the beach, on 138th Street in Belle Harbor. Rockaway Beach was our backyard. I could jump off the deck onto the beach. I loved the feeling of sand in my sheets. The first official day of summer would always be when I ran the length of my beach and dove into the Atlantic.

As I grew older, Anna tailored all of my clothes. I can still picture her kneeling before me, uttering with needles in her mouth, "Is that good, sweetie?" Anna lived a long, healthy life. She worked until she was seventy-eight and cooked for her great-grand-children, who still talk about her meatballs. In early October 2012, at age ninety-five, Anna passed away.

Three weeks later, Hurricane Sandy was rapidly heading toward New York. My parents were still living in the house where I grew up and, like most die-hard Rockaway folks, didn't want to evacuate.

My brother, my children, and I begged them to stay with my family in Brooklyn for the night. They finally relented and drove over with nothing more than a change of clothes and toiletries.

Sandy struck Rockaway hard. Early the morning after, my parents and I drove toward home. We blew through the Marine Parkway Bridge before it was even reopened. Cars were abandoned. Houses were a mess. Neighbors were roaming the streets like zombies. We maneuvered down 138th Street, slowly, and fifty feet away from the beach, I got out of the car by myself to look. Sandy had ripped away half of our house, as if she had swiped her massive arm from the beach side and scooped out everything she wanted. The entire side of the house was exposed for the world to see. It was crushing. My parents walked up to the house and were horrified. We hugged, talked, cried, and eventually drove somberly back to Brooklyn.

My parents stayed with us for a week or so. We all mourned together. My wife, Stacey, took care of us all. My dad then decided he and my mom would live in Anna's house in Queens until they figured out what they should do next. Even after her death, Anna was still taking care of her boy.

Our Rockaway house was condemned. No one was allowed in. From the beach, we could see my father's second floor closet ripped open, but not completely destroyed. In the closet you could see his ties, including Anna's. Weeks later, despite many warnings, my dad's friend ventured in and retrieved some valuables, including a bunch of Anna's ties.

That day, my father came over to my house, smiling for what seemed like the first time since the storm. He proudly presented me with two of Anna's ties. I wear them all the time. I like handling the silk as I knot the ties. Even so, if you see me in one of Anna's ties and you fancy it, compliment me on it. I just may take it off and give it to you.

Ross Intelisano is a Queens-boy who lives in Brooklyn and practices law in Manhattan.

Niki Russ Federman

I spent a lot of time at Russ & Daughters growing up. The earliest job I can remember giving myself was when I was about five years old. I would wait by the store entrance for the produce deliveries to arrive. The delivery guys would wheel in fifty-pound bags of potatoes, onions, and carrots with hand trucks, and I would jump on top of those sacks and direct them to the kitchen. I felt very important.

When I wasn't doing this "work," I would run behind the side of the store where there were bins filled with all kinds of candies. I would go down the line of bins and just fill my pockets. We sold those coffee nibs that my grandmother always had in her apartment, and still does. You'd eat those candies and your upper and lower jaws would get stuck together.

My father, who took over the business from my grandparents, liked to show me off to the customers. I'd answer the phone and everyone thought that was cute. During the Jewish holidays, which are the busiest times, I would help out behind the counter. Just like my dad, if I was working I'd wear a white coat. Everyone who was working did. For one hundred years, everyone always has.

I left the store for a while. I went to college, and then worked at a museum in San Francisco and a United Nations nonprofit. Subconsciously, I now realize, I was trying to get as far away from the business as I could. In 2001, though, seeing the need to improve the store's terribly basic website, I offered to work for my father on this one project. My father, however, took my entrance as his exit, his salvation. Very quickly he wanted me to decide whether I would take over Russ & Daughters. There was no middle ground. It was a tortured couple of years because the thing I knew I loved was getting tainted, like I was being forced into an arranged marriage. At that point, entering the

family business wouldn't have been because it was something I wanted to do. It would have been because it was expected of me. I saw doing the very thing that my great-grandparents, my grandparents, and my parents did as a failure.

Being a fishmonger was not a path I had expected to fall into, so in a dark moment, and to buy myself some time and space, I enrolled in business school. By the second day I knew it wasn't the right fit.

By then I'd had an opportunity to think about the meaning of Russ & Daughters. Following in the footsteps of three prior generations of my family was actually not a suffocating thing; it was, instead, this special, powerful legacy, and also a great challenge—how to maintain the very authenticity and tradition of a business with such social currency and history, and then to make it grow. Because I had consciously stepped away, it was then my choice to come back. I joined my cousin and we became the fourth generation of the Russ family to own and operate the business.

I recently brought my two-year-old daughter into the store. In my mind, I had envisioned her getting used to the store and the smells just as I had, saying hello to all of the customers, and everyone getting soft and fuzzy. I could just imagine her running up and down the store, eating a bagel and a pickle. Instead, she came in, saw me, and everyone around her, in white coats, and had a meltdown. The white coats, it turns out, reminded her of a trip to the hospital that had taken place a few months prior. She started ripping the coat off of me, saying, "No, no, no, no!" My whole dream of the story didn't go as expected.

Who knows, though? Perhaps one day she'll get over her fear of white coats and be the fifth generation of Russ & Daughters to put one on.

—AS TOLD TO EMILY SPIVACK

Niki Russ Federman is a fourth-generation owner of Russ & Daughters in New York.

Brian Balderston

I knew something was wrong the moment I walked inside the house. I'd been working as a project manager for a guy who renovated houses in Washington, D.C., and I was dropping off a small crew to do demolition on the downstairs apartment for the owners who lived in the upstairs apartment. The door was ajar, like it had been forced open, and I heard something upstairs, but I knew no one was supposed to be home.

I told the two people with me to grab sledgehammers and crowbars from the car in case we needed weapons. I could hear someone scurrying around. I shouted that he needed to come down. I paused. No answer. I yelled that we were coming up. "I'm coming downstairs and I have a gun!" he yelled back. He was just repeating it over and over, "I have a gun! I have a gun!" If he had a gun, I was stepping aside, I thought, as I looked at the crowbar I was holding.

Because of the layout of the space, I couldn't really see him until he was eight or ten feet away from me. I saw that he didn't have a gun but that he had a knife, something he must have found rummaging through kitchen drawers for a weapon. At that point, he lunged at me. I instinctively raised my arms to protect myself, and he knocked me backward.

The guy stood up and tried to hurdle over me. But I had two guys with me, construction dudes. One was a big Honduran guy who was born on a ranch and the other guy was from New Zealand and played rugby. You don't fuck with these guys. So mid-hurdle, the Honduran grabbed the burglar and body slammed him. The burglar got back up. The rugby player kicked him down. I saw one of the construction guys standing over the attacker with a pickax. He must have realized that if he swung that thing, he was going to kill the guy because he paused. At that moment, the burglar jumped up and started to run away.

By then I had my bearings, and I took the crowbar and threw it down the street at him. It was like the movies; it got the guy in the legs and he went down. The rugby player grabbed the crowbar and chased him until they reached an alley, at which point the rugby player saw that the burglar had another couple of knives, like he was ready to battle, and decided it was probably best not to pursue him any longer.

While that was happening, I realized I was bleeding. I started feeling warmth on my body but I couldn't feel pain anywhere, so I didn't know if I had been stabbed in the arm or the ribs or the stomach. I just felt warmth.

It was February, so it was cold, and we were all standing outside. I was wearing a jacket along with a gray zip-up shirt that is typically for running or biking. I looked down and saw a big bloodstain on the arm of my jacket. It was when I saw the blood seeping through my coat sleeve that I knew I had been stabbed in the arm.

The ambulance took me to Howard University Hospital, and I got seven or eight stitches. It could have been much worse: what if I hadn't raised my arms in self-defense when the guy lunged at me?

I threw away the coat because it was drenched with blood, but I kept the shirt because I was able to wash out the stain. Even though it still has that one-inch slit in the arm—the point of entry where the guy got me—it's still wearable, so why get rid of it? It's Patagonia and that stuff lasts forever.

—AS TOLD TO EMILY SPIVACK

Brian Balderston is a Brooklyn-based artist and cofounder of Present Company.

Margaret D. Stetz

"Oh, I remember you. You're the woman with the ears." I've heard this often at social and professional gatherings. Not that there's anything unusual about the appendages—pale, fleshy, and half-hidden by a mop of curls—on either side of my face. The ears that leave such a lasting impression aren't attached to my head, however, but to a headband. They're white and fuzzy on the outside, a satiny pink on the inside, and measure about six-inches long when standing erect, though they can be bent or tilted at a jaunty angle. And they're not on view all the time, but come out mainly when I'm giving public lectures that have something to do with Beatrix Potter, the British children's book author and artist whose work is one of my academic specialties. Sometimes, depending on the time of day, they get replaced by the pair that I call "Evening Ears," which are entirely white and ornamented with sequins, so that they appear a bit more formal (or at least sparkly and festive).

Why would a middle-aged professor of women's studies and literature—with a PhD from Harvard, no less—be wearing these? I have a list of reasonable-sounding excuses. Giving a talk means I'm supposed to be the center of attention, and the ears certainly help to focus the audience on my speech. Especially now, when people sitting in lecture halls have an array of electronic distractions in their laps, there's nothing like the sight of bunny ears accompanying a woman's sober business suit to make them look up from their screens. Obviously, too, if my subject is Beatrix Potter, creator of the immortal Peter Rabbit, a pair of long ears serves as a visual tribute.

But here's my confession: I *like* wearing them, and, if I had the courage, I'd probably do so more often—maybe all the time. As with the old feminist adage, "The personal is political," my attraction to those rabbit ears on a headband is both personal and political, and the two motives weigh equally.

The political angle is easier to explain. Both sets of ears came from a drugstore's post-Halloween discount aisle and were intended to top off adult party costumes (low-cut bodysuits, fishnets, high heels, etc.). The notion of dressing women as "Bunnies" was, of course, the invention of Hugh Hefner's Playboy Clubs. When she was a young journalist, *Ms.* magazine founder Gloria Steinem famously went undercover as a Bunny in 1963 to expose the harassment and miserable working conditions of women who wore the Clubs' uniforms. Today, there's something satisfying about taking these symbols of sexual availability and servility and flipping their meaning. By combining bunny ears with a tailored jacket and skirt on the lecture platform at a university, museum, or other cultural institution, I'm doing something subversive. No longer do they signify that women are merely "Playmates." Conversely, this is also my way of suggesting that women don't have to be wholly serious to be feminists. Feminists know how to take or make a joke and even enjoy being silly, as I do, with what they wear.

But there's more to it. I'm drawn to rabbits, especially wild ones. The way they look and move thrills me. They're funny, yet dignified—cuddly, but wary. They know that they are prey living in a world of predators, so they leap and cavort, but always with their eyes open and their ears up. When I put on that headband to lecture, my ears are up, too. I don't become a rabbit; I become more myself. And maybe that's really what makes people remember the ears—and me.

Margaret D. Stetz is a writer and professor of women's studies and humanities at the University of Delaware.

Rosanne Cash

I keep clothing from people I love in my closet with the rest of my clothes. Like the scarf with "Mom" knitted into it, made by my daughter Chelsea several years ago. Or my mom's sweatshirts and yoga pants and nightgown, which I keep in the drawer with my own nightgowns.

In my closet, hanging with my blouses, there's a shirt of my dad's. I don't do anything special with it. It was such an unusual shirt for him; it's bright purple with tuxedo pleats down the front, so different from his uniform of black shirts and black jackets, although he did wear it on-stage a few times.

My dad died in 2003, and each of his children got some of his clothing. I got his heavy gray coats, some stage jackets, a pair of really nice boots that I'm saving for my son, and a couple of odd things, like one of his J. Peterman khaki jackets that he used to wear in Jamaica.

When we were going through his things, I didn't have a clear reason for taking this purple tuxedo shirt. My dad was a very big man, so the shirt is absolutely enormous on me, but once in a while I'll put it on. Sometimes when I look at the jackets and the boots, it makes me very sad and I miss him. I think of his big feet and those big boots. But I look at the purple shirt and I smile.

I'll pass this shirt along to my son, Jake, who was only four when his grandpa died. He's going to be a large man like my dad and the only one who the shirt will fit.

—AS TOLD TO EMILY SPIVACK

Rosanne Cash is a singer-songwriter and author.

David Carr

I live in the New Jersey suburbs where the morning weather often bears little or no relation to what the weather might be like in the afternoon in New York, where I work. Many days I have miscalculated my clothing needs for the day—in part because I work in Midtown in a forest of tall buildings, and if there is a chill in the air it is multiplied by the wind that becomes amplified and focused by the canyon of structures around me.

I generally deal with the dissonance by refusing to go outside or by grabbing a fake cashmere scarf for five bucks off the street vendor tables in Times Square. I think there is a direct relationship between what you pay for an item and how long you hang on to it, so those scarves tend to come and go. (Though I do have a watch I bought on Canal Street almost a decade ago for five bucks and it is still with me. I wear it every day and replace the battery every few years for more than the cost of the watch. But that's a different story.) Even if they last, I am a spiller, so they become a sort of napkin-cravat after a while and my wife quietly retires them without telling me.

On a very hot day last summer, I had the opposite problem. I left for work dressed for a rare television shoot, which means that I had put on a sport coat and dress shirt with a tie on top, and wore the usual black jeans and sneakers on bottom. After work, I was meeting a pal at the Frying Pan, which is a bar on a no-longer-seaworthy boat off of a pier in Chelsea.

The bar is aptly named. On a sunny day, the light and heat reflecting off the water mean that the people on the boat are slowly sautéed. Yes, a sunset on the Hudson is an amazing thing, so spectacular that even my home state of New Jersey looks majestic, but it can get very hot out there. It's also worth mentioning that Manhattan itself throws off a fair amount of heat because of the so-called heat island effect.

It was still very hot when I left my office at the end of the day, and even though I left behind my sport coat the sun immediately absorbed into the dark dress shirt I was wearing, so I walked down the street to the tourists' shops of Times Square for any old T-shirt that I could wear. Even at six bucks a pop, they were hideous, all of them swaddled in the announcement that the wearer was in fact, or had once been, on a particular island off the coast of America called New York.

I was just about to give up. My fading hipster cred—already suffering many hellacious blows because of advancing age—would not allow me to wear a shirt suggesting that "I ♥ New York." You can't wear a shirt like that ironically unless, say, you hate New York, which I do not. I still have an immigrant's ardor for the place, having come here a decade ago for a job. Before my family joined me, I lived in Tribeca for a few months. My second day in New York, I rode my bike into a fence at Broadway and Canal because I was looking up at a pair of tall buildings downtown. Those buildings are now gone, but the wonder, the sense of awe at traveling through one of humankind's greatest creations, remains.

And then I saw one—extra-large, thank god—in which the classic New York script had been misprinted upside down. I knew what to do. I turned to the guy running the shop and said, "This one is a misprint. I'll give you three bucks." He said nothing, but nodded. I paid in two crumpled bills and quarters, ducked behind a rack, and put it on. As soon as I stepped out on the street, people stared. I got on the C train to 23rd, and a kid next to me stared at the logo over my burgeoning middle-aged midsection and said, "I like your shirt."

"Thanks, man. Three bucks."

Whenever I wear the shirt in New York, waitresses, bartenders, cab drivers, they all say nice things about the shirt and ignore the fact that the rack it's hanging on could use some work. When

I travel, which is fairly often, and wear the shirt, which is less often, nobody ever says anything. I like that about my shirt: it is something that is intuitively understood in the City, as we insufferable locals call it, and is baffling to others, akin to many other aspects of living or working in New York.

I daydreamed for a while about getting some pals of my wife in the clothing business to crank out a few hundred. I even had a slogan for the back: "Turning New York upside down one shirt at a time." But then someone in the business explained to me that you couldn't trademark the idea of turning lettering someone else created upside down. So I just wear mine instead.

It won't last. It's white, for one thing, and a series of small food and beverage disasters have already begun to dapple its surface. One day, it will accumulate enough stains and history so that it will mysteriously disappear from my drawer. I will miss it.

David Carr is an author and works for the *New York Times* as a media columnist and culture reporter.

Ariel Schrag & Matt Wolf

ARIEL SCHRAG: My friends and I used to walk up and down Telegraph Avenue buying T-shirts, weed patches, and herbal cigarettes. I wanted to be this tough skater, so all my clothes were really big and baggy: giant shredded jeans with fishnets underneath, Airwalks, and suspenders. I loved the suspender look but when you have breasts, where do your suspenders go? Girls can't really wear suspenders if they have anything above a negative A-cup. Otherwise, the suspenders are always askew or around one breast or pushing to both sides or in the middle or awkwardly rubbing against your nipples. My baggy look only lasted a little while. Then I went straight into the No Doubt–Gwen Stefani look and I would wear these wife beaters, wing tips, and brown slacks.

This Puma T-shirt came from the store Wasteland. I bought it during my skater-goth phase before I switched to the No Doubt ska look. I really loved it, but after a couple of months of wear it just felt like it was too big. I sold it back to Wasteland, probably to buy some No Doubt stuff, a five-pack of wife beaters, or hair bleach. Funds were limited so this shirt had to go, but it was one of those shirts I always remembered missing after I had given it away.

MATT WOLF: Ariel was way cooler than I was in high school. She was a notable gay teenager in Berkeley and a few years older than me. I knew of her through her comic character. I was an over-achieving gay activist who self-identified as a gay separatist in school because I didn't have any friends.

I got involved with this gay activist organization in San Francisco and would use it as an excuse to take the CalTrain into the city every week from San Jose. I'd go to an hour-and-a-half meeting and then walk around the city with a fictional purpose because I wanted to be cosmopolitan. I would take the bus to Haight Street and go to the thrift stores. As I was defining my edge, as one might say, I would wear baggy jeans with No Fear or Gumby T-shirts and dog tags. It was around that time that I realized it was cooler to wear old stuff, even if it didn't really fit, and that's when I started shopping at thrift stores in San Francisco.

AS: Late one perfect summer night about six months ago, I walked into the Graham Avenue Deli in Williamsburg, Brooklyn, and Matt was in the bodega. He and I had become friends over the years and we lived in the same neighborhood. That night I immediately recognized that he was wearing my Puma shirt.

MW: Ariel was like, "Hey, Matt! Wait a minute. What are you wearing?" I was stoned at the deli, looking for sugar-free chocolate, so my response time was slow.

AS: And I felt stoned because he was wearing my shirt. It had been out of my life for a decade or two, but I knew it instantly. I told him, "I used to have a shirt just like that when I was in high school, but I got rid of it. I gave it away to Wasteland." He told me he'd bought it in high school at Wasteland.

I'm neurotic and don't like the feel of tags on my skin so I cut them out of my shirts. It's very likely I cut the tag off this T-shirt, which is why there's a hole in the neck. And the side of the shirt is shredded because all my shirts at the time would get caught on my studded belt and rip. There's no question of whether it had been mine.

MW: It is one of my only thrift store purchases that actually fit me. And one of the only pieces of clothing I held on to from high school. I always feel awkward and uncomfortable in whatever I'm wearing. It's normal for my clothes not to fit right, but I wear this T-shirt constantly because I love it so much. It's soft, perfectly threadbare but not see-through, and I think I look good in it.

AS: And that's what killed me—how good Matt looked in it that night at the bodega. It was everything I couldn't be as this awkward teenage girl with breasts and suspenders, wearing a too-big T-shirt. And then there's Matt, a man, and the shirt falls just right on his chest. I wanted to tell him to give me the shirt back. Instead, I walked home from the deli and emailed him a photo of my midnineties, purple-haired teenage self, sitting on a curb in my baggy jeans with a skateboard on my lap, staring at the camera, wearing that T-shirt.

—AS TOLD TO EMILY SPIVACK

Ariel Schrag is a Brooklyn-based author of the novel *Adam* and the graphic memoirs *Awkward and Definition*, *Potential*, and *Likewise*.

Matt Wolf is a New York–based filmmaker whose films include *Teenage* and *Wild Combination: A Portrait of Arthur Russell*.

Kelly Jones

A few weeks shy of my twentieth birthday, in 2004, I moved to New Orleans. Shortly thereafter, one of my best friends came to visit. We played tourist and partied on and off Bourbon Street. In a run-down gift shop we stumbled into, we discovered a back room full of cheap blouses and hippie skirts. I bought this batik tie-dye wrap skirt for ten dollars.

The first time I wore the skirt was a few weeks later. I was in New York for the Republican National Convention protests, documenting a march I had helped organize. In my downtime I was exploring the city, and at dusk I wound up walking alone through Central Park. There I encountered a group of pagans at the edge of the park. They were holding hands and dancing in a circle. A man on the end of the spiral locked eyes with me, extended his arm my way, and said, "Join us." For some reason, I did. And we twirled about in the park, stopping eventually to light candles and pray for peace.

A couple years later, I was living in Asheville, North Carolina, spending my time waiting tables at a Cajun pub downtown while trying to decide if I wanted to go back to college or do something else with my life. One night I was in front of the restaurant on a smoke break, wearing my batik skirt. As I was putting out my cigarette to go back inside, coincidentally, my best guy friend from high school walked out of the bar next door. He dropped his beer and picked me up, twirling me around a few times before placing my feet back on the sidewalk. It was a slow night, so I stayed outside chatting for a while. He told me he was in town for final training before redeploying to Iraq for his second tour. I got the address of the hotel where he was staying and promised to meet him at the bar there a few hours later. We stayed up late drinking Long Island Iced Teas. He got sloshy and dropped a lit cigarette in my lap, leaving a small burn stain on the skirt. Two days later he was shipped out.

After Asheville, I moved to Seattle to finish college. On a warm spring day I pulled my skirt out of the closet and wore it around town. A stranger at a coffee shop came up to me and asked me out. This happened frequently when I wore this skirt; men were strangely attracted to what was slowly becoming a cheap, stained rag. It was ripped from biking in it, stained in spots, and marred by a couple burn holes that were quite noticeable. I thanked him for his attention and politely declined. That night, still in my favorite skirt, I checked my email and found out that my friend had died in Iraq.

Kelly Jones is a New Orleans–based writer who makes a living as a writing tutor, bartender, and web content ghostwriter.

Brandi Chastain

This T-shirt is from the first soccer tournament I played in, the Redwood Classic in Sebastopol, California. It was 1979 and I was ten years old. Driving to the tournament felt like we were going somewhere really special, like we were traveling across the Earth, because we crossed the Golden Gate Bridge. Really, though, we only drove an hour and fifteen minutes from my parents' house in San Jose to get to this weekend-long tournament.

My soccer team's name was the Horizon and my dad was the coach. He was my coach my entire youth soccer, career, from the time I was nine until I was sixteen years old. He didn't know anything about soccer, so we learned together. We went to the library, got books, watched videos, and had season tickets to the Earthquakes.

It was an interesting time for soccer. It was seen as a foreign sport, so there was a lot of international influence. At the same time, soccer had just started to get a foothold in what was called the North American Soccer League. This was the era when Pelé played for the New York Cosmos.

It was the perfect storm; I started playing a game that had just begun an American league with these international stars that had played in the World Cups and European Cups. I got hooked. And luckily for me, I grew up in California in a neighborhood where people were cool about trying everything. It was a very encouraging and familial environment; in addition to my dad acting as my coach, my mom was the quintessential soccer mom, yelling through the megaphone from the sidelines (she was also a bit of a pack rat and saved this T-shirt for me). My teammates were all my neighbors, and they felt like my sisters. It was a special time. I've been around the world and played in really big games, but that was one of my favorite moments playing soccer.

One of the reasons that the Redwood Classic was so memorable was that the tournament also hosted a juggling contest. I had soccer practice twice a week and I was with the ball a little bit every day until my mom would call me in for dinner. But I was also really excited about juggling. I would practice in my free time: in my house, in my backyard, at school. It was the first time I saw myself as a young girl trying to get better at something because I really wanted to do well in the juggling contest.

We probably came in second or third or fourth in the soccer tournament. I actually don't remember. I do remember that in between games, the juggling contest took place. Somewhere there's a photograph where I'm wearing the tournament T-shirt and holding two ribbons. One was for soccer and the other one was for juggling. I came in seventh place.

—AS TOLD TO EMILY SPIVACK

Brandi Chastain is a professional soccer player who has won two Women's World Cup championships, two Olympic gold medals, and an Olympic silver medal.

Jeff Zimbalist

Shortly after I arrived in India, I made my way to the Maha Kumbh Mela, a Hindu gathering in Allahabad that happens once every 144 years when the planets align in such a way that they point to an intersection of the Ganges, the Yamuna, and Saraswati rivers. According to Hindu tradition, it's believed that if you bathe in the rivers' intersection at sunrise on that specific day, then you receive *amrita*—the nectar of immortality—and you're freed from the cycle of life and death.

I was living with the Rainbow Gathering while I was at the Kumbh Mela. I had these wicked long dreadlocks and a hammock that I had made out of a piece of cloth and string. I ate free meals that the Hare Krishnas gave out. I had a crush on this girl who sang Hindu chants on the other side of the bonfire every night. Everyone was stroking each other with love and spiritual guidance, and it was just fucking beautiful.

I met this American journalist, Rob, and I found out that we were going on the same two-week silent meditation retreat. I'd admired his shirt, which he had custom made at a local tailor; I just thought it was dope. We hung out all afternoon and we bathed together at the intersection of the rivers at sundown. Afterward, he gave me his shirt. I'd been shirtless at the Maha Kumbh Mela, but after that, I wore it every day.

The meditation retreat at the Thai temple in Bodh Gaya was otherworldly, in-sync-with-the-cosmos-type shit. It was like being thrust into the professional level of a certain culture that I knew very little about, having skipped the minor leagues to get there. The lesson that came out of the retreat was rooted in Vipassana, the breath, and the ability to breathe through any experience; that becomes your shield.

After the retreat, I split off from Rob and made friends with an English-speaking rickshaw driver. I hung out with him for a couple days in Jaipur, and we established a rapport.

I had traveler's checks and needed to exchange money. I knew I'd get a better rate on the black market, so I asked the rickshaw driver if he knew anyone. He took me to a little jewelry shop on a cobblestone street. The guys were friendly and they gave me a good rate. They asked if I'd like to go out with them that evening. I didn't want to say no to an adventure. They told me I needed to clean myself up because they were taking me to a fancy place. They bought me a pair of shiny silver suit pants, shoes, and a belt. I wore the shirt that Rob had given me, tucked into the suit pants. I pulled back my dreadlocks.

That night was straight gangster cliché. We went to a nondescript building, through a cellar door, down stairs, and through a bustling, smoky kitchen. At the end of the kitchen, a door led to a strip club with really nasty looking strippers. Guys were making it rain rupees. We got hammered and afterward my rickshaw driver took me back to my hotel. It was super fun, so I hung out with them again the next night.

On the second night they said, "The reason we've been courting you is because we have a proposition." They went on to explain that, in India, you're only allowed to export a certain amount of jewelry each year to the U.S. without having to pay a tariff, but that on a U.S. passport, you could bring up to an additional $20,000 worth of purchased goods into the U.S. They asked if I would take jewelry back to the U.S., or mail it to myself and drop it off at a jeweler in New York City. I'd get $20,000 and they'd sell the jewelry for $90,000. I told them I wasn't interested a number of times, but they urged me to call former backpackers who'd done it, a Brit and an American, who were very convincing. Eventually, I decided it was a no-risk situation, and while I wasn't in a materialistic state of mind at that point, I thought I'd buy my mom the hot tub she'd always wanted.

Since I didn't want to carry the jewels on my person I put them in a package and the guys took me to a post office, where I mailed them to my mom's house in Massachusetts. As soon as I did that, things changed. I got picked up by two massive angry-looking dudes who didn't speak English, in a car I'd never seen before. And they had my bag in the car! Since the rickshaw driver knew where I was staying, he had taken my bag from the hotel and signed me out. The two guys in the car said that their boss didn't trust me and that I needed to fly with them to Mumbai to convince their boss that everything was okay. I told them I didn't want to go, of course. Tensions were rising, and I was in a tough situation because they could have been armed. I reminded myself that I had this tool, the breath, Vipassana, an idealistic philosophy that I could breathe through it.

I finally relented, and we took a private plane to Bombay where we were picked up by a driver. I rode in a car with three guys who spoke no English for an hour and a half through the Bombay night. They took me to the penthouse of a crappy hotel where I wound up bunking with the two guys, who stayed in the room with me at all times. I wasn't allowed to leave except to go to the hotel restaurant, where a few times a day the boss would show up and tell me I needed to put a $20,000 deposit on my credit card before they could let me go. He said his guys had been too trusting and had sent the jewels too soon. He wasn't sure if I would rob them or actually take the jewels to New York.

I realized the irony of the situation. It was 180 degrees from staring across the bonfire at the dreadlock girl at the Rainbow Gathering on top of the hill, under the trees and stars, singing Hindu chants at Kumbh Mela.

On the third morning I snuck out of the hotel while the guys were still sleeping. I found a call center and called my credit card company. I spoke to two representatives who assured me that the credit card company would cover me on misrepresentation of merchandise because they personally approve each of their vendors across the world. I got off the phone thinking, "Fuck it. If the credit card company is willing to take the risk, I need to get the hell out of here."

Since I didn't have my own credit card at the time, they ran my mom's credit card. She'd given it to me for emergencies only. Even though I have a high tolerance for risk, I figured I'd been kidnapped for three days, and that this was an emergency. I signed over the maximum on the card, $16,100.

And in no time, I was on a plane heading back to the States with all my stuff, still wearing the same shirt Rob had given me at the Kumbh Mela. They even paid for my ticket out of Bombay. I was sitting on the flight thinking that everything might be okay—they had just dropped a thousand dollars to fly me home, bought me clothes, put me up in a hotel, and were all smiles and hugs, reassuring me.

I got home and the jewels arrived on schedule. I immediately got them appraised. They were worth $2,500, not $20,000. And then my mom's credit card was charged $16,100. When I called the credit card company, they said to look at the fine print. They would only cover misrepresentation within a one hundred mile radius of one's billing address, never mind another hemisphere.

At that point, I had to admit to my mom that I'd been scammed. All my pride in being able to survive anywhere, all the years traveling in Latin America, and all the spiritual highs of my semi-enlightened self in India came crashing down into a harsh reality.

I cut my dreadlocks off, bought a suit from Goodwill, and went to the local law library in the basement of a church in Northampton. I asked them to take me to the consumer protection section and I spent two weeks asking questions of paralegals, lawyers, and law librarians. One day when I came into the library, one of the law librarians was holding up a manila folder of printouts like it was the fucking *Pelican Brief*. She told me she'd found a relevant case that had been settled out of court.

That information was enough for me to get a pro bono attorney. My attorney put together a brief and sent it to the bank. The bank pushed back a couple of times with settlement offers, but we didn't take any of them. The statute of limitations has now expired for the case, and although I have no idea what to do with them I still have the jewels.

I had a tremendously romantic affair with India before it broke my heart, but I've chosen to love it again. In fact, I've been back a few times. I have always sought the spirit I had during that trip; that's part of the reason why I've held on to this shirt. Because I'd like to think I can still summon the total carpe diem, reckless abandon, bulletproof sense of invincibility that I once had wearing that shirt.

—AS TOLD TO EMILY SPIVACK

Jeff Zimbalist is a filmmaker whose films include *Favela Rising*, *The Two Escobars*, *Youngstown Boys*, *Bollywood: The Greatest Love Story Ever Told*, and *Pelé—Birth of the Legend*.

Jill Meisner

In the 1970s my grandfather, Murray Meisner, was called "the man who dressed New York." Through the seventies and part of the eighties, his eponymous womens wear company was known for its practical dresses. They were sold at J.C. Penney and Sears, to secretaries and other working women. One denim dress he designed became so popular that he had to move all the company's manufacturing to China to keep up with the demand—that was a really big deal back then.

My dad would take me to visit my grandfather at his office in the garment district. My grandfather was always so proud of his grandchildren, and he'd parade me around the office to meet his employees, which, when I was young, felt like so many people. During one visit in the early eighties, when I was four or five years old, I told my grandfather that I wanted to be Minnie Mouse for Halloween. Since they had sewers on-site, they made me a costume on the spot, a red and white apron with ruffles that Minnie Mouse would wear. I loved it.

One day, sometime in 2003, I was bored at work and I googled my grandfather. I found a few of his dresses for sale on eBay, Etsy, and an online vintage boutique. I started buying the ones I could imagine wearing. That began my Murray Meisner dress collection.

I have six now. When I told my grandfather I was collecting his dresses, he thought it was hysterical. "You're doing what? Your grandmother would have a heart attack if she knew," he told me. My grandmother had been one of those New York women who lived on the Upper East Side and didn't work. She'd never consider wearing one of her husband's dresses. She wore almost exclusively Chanel. And every Saturday she'd walk up and down Fifth Avenue window-shopping. I guess you could say she was sort of snobby, but there was more to her than that.

In 2004 I started my own company, which required a more professional look. I had to go from dressing like a kid to dressing like an adult. And so, strangely, I found myself—as thousands of women had decades before me—slipping into Murray Meisner originals to head to the office.

—AS TOLD TO EMILY SPIVACK

Jill Meisner is the director of public relations for Refinery29.

Kenneth Goldsmith

In 2011 I was invited to the White House to read poetry for President Obama's "Celebration of American Poetry." During the day I did a poetry workshop with Michelle Obama for seventy high school students in the State Dining Room, and in the evening I did a formal reading in the East Room, where I read traffic reports to the President of the United States. Of course, the biggest question was what I would wear.

My suit was designed by the avant-garde designer Thom Browne, under his Brooks Brothers–owned Black Fleece label. He pretty much does what I was doing by reading traffic reports at the White House: he takes the traditional patterns that Brooks Brothers is known for—in this case paisley—and pushes them way too far. (Coincidentally, Obama was also wearing a Brooks Brothers suit when he met me, but of a very different sort.) During the day session with the First Lady, I wore a Thom Browne pastel suit, which references the insane pastels of the preppy Newport set. For this suit, Brown created a pastiche or patchwork of traditional preppy colors and literally made a remix of them.

It was clear that Brooks Brothers needed to revitalize its brand, shake up the staid traditions, hence Browne was called in to bring the company into the twenty-first century and to add a big dose of *impurity*. Clearly that meant not ditching its classic line but spinning off another line based on what it had become famous for.

I figured that the Obamas—preps to the core— would in some way recognize the paisley and the pastels, but be befuddled by the size of the paisley or the way that the pastels were unconventionally stitched together. And that, in fact, was the case. Upon our introduction, the first thing the President said to me was, "That's a great suit! You know? I'd wear a suit like that. But my staff would never let me." To which I replied, "Mr. President, this is one instance where it's better being an artist than being the President of the United States: artists can wear anything they want." And then he glanced down at my saddle shoes and exclaimed, "You're wearing golf shoes!" Which in part was true, that being the genius of Thom Browne, to take something familiar and recontextualize it to the point of it being "wrong." And that is exactly what I aimed to do with my performance: to straddle tradition and radicality, being both and, at the same time, being neither; to embrace contradiction, keep people guessing.

That evening Jon Stewart took the piss out of me on *The Daily Show*: "American poets, young and old, spoke out at the White House tonight about a variety of subjects from support for public libraries to memories of a favorite teacher to how hard it is to find a nice blazer on short notice. Uh…it's tonight? Does that wallpaper come off?"

A year and a half later, Thom Browne exploded across the world when it was revealed that he designed Michelle Obama's 2013 inauguration dress. I like to think that I played some small part in that decision.

Kenneth Goldsmith is a poet, founding editor of *UbuWeb*, and the first
Poet Laureate at the Museum of Modern Art in New York.

Pat Mahoney

LCD Soundsystem never had a uniform or a cool look onstage. We all looked like substitute teachers: jeans, sweaters, T-shirts, sneakers.

When we started out, we had a half hour's worth of music to play live. Then the shows gradually got longer and more intense, and turned into these epic sets. I sweat a lot in general, but during those shows, I would sweat so profusely that my jeans would be drenched and I'd be soaked to the bone.

After a show, I'd hang my jeans up to dry in the tour bus, but people would get upset because it smelled really bad, like rotten cotton. I tried drying them in the cargo area of the bus but mold colonies grew on them. This was when we had relatively few creature comforts, and we didn't get to do laundry that much.

I needed a solution—something that would dry quickly and not rot—so I went to American Apparel and bought a pair of flesh-colored nylon short shorts. I thought I'd wear them as a joke— you know, to wind people up. But it also totally improved the bus/clothing situation. Because they were made of nylon, I could wash them with hand soap, ring them out, and hang them up on the bus to dry, and the next day they would be fine. And if I draped them over the door of the bathroom backstage and we rolled out without them, I could always replace them with another pair because there's an American Apparel in every major city in the world.

The shorts had the added bonus of coming in almost my exact flesh color, so if we were playing a massive festival where people were a hundred yards back, it looked like I came onstage with no clothes on. Fans came to expect them. When I walked out onstage in my tiny shorts, I got a little cheer. I'm shy but I have quite an exhibitionist streak, and I like to do things for a laugh.

I have always had terrible stage fright. Once I play the first note of the first song, I'm fine, but before that, I can get paralytically afraid. The only way I could overcome the fear was to make sure that everything was the same every night. I'm not a baseball fan, but the other day I was at a Red Sox game and one of the batters had this elaborate juju that he did with his batting helmet and gloves. He had to have everything just right so he could hit the ball. Each time before we played, I had to make sure my sneakers were tied just right, that the seat was just so, that my drums went exactly where they'd been marked on the rug. And although my shorts were very much the opposite of armor, they also became part of the ritual. I might have been tired or my hands might have hurt or I might have been hungover, but at least my clothing and physical proximity to the drums was always the same. Knowing that I was going to be comfortable to play for two to three hours was hugely important. Then I could launch right into it.

—AS TOLD TO EMILY SPIVACK

Pat Mahoney was a founding member and drummer for LCD Soundsystem and is lead vocalist for Museum of Love.

Laura Jane Kenny

I have a small collection of men's garments that I've acquired from one-night stands. I've never taken something that wasn't given to me. Yet, whether I'm handed an extra T-shirt to sleep in or a scarf to wear home, I've managed to accumulate dating memorabilia and I don't know what to do with them.

I'm not a hoarder. I clean out my wardrobe diligently every six months. Yet I keep the remains of these escapades neatly tucked away in the back of my closet, empty shells of late nights and questionable decisions that evolved into nothing at all.

The first piece of clothing I ever kept was that of a young man named Roger, whom I met at a sports bar. I left his apartment early on the morning that followed our long night—a pitiful but endearing pickup line, endless cheap drinks, a late-night invitation, and an even later-night acceptance. After I finished getting dressed, Roger gave me an extra-large, royal blue sweatshirt that was soft from frequent washing and had sleeves that were so long that only the tips of my fingers peeked out from the cuffs. He deposited the sweatshirt into my arms and kindly told me I would need it. It was April and still fairly chilly in the morning. Roger asked me to give it back to him the next time I saw him. He walked me to the front door and as he kissed me goodbye, I was acutely aware that I did not have his phone number nor did he have mine.

I remember it was Palm Sunday. As I headed to the train, dozens of people were walking to church in pastel-colored clothes, carrying dead palm leaves that swept the sidewalk. I was far out in Brooklyn, and my very presence, that of a tall, blonde twenty-something, was so out of place that two different people stopped me to ask if I was lost. I consulted Google Maps as I walked to an unknown train stop. I kept my head down with my hair piled into a bun and my body wrapped in a stranger's sweatshirt that I would never wear again.

Maybe it wasn't even his sweatshirt. It could have been a roommate's or the remnants of some party. Maybe Roger thought the sweatshirt would pacify any requests for phone numbers or doubts regarding his follow-up. Perhaps he felt guilty that I would be cold, that I had traveled all the way into the depths of Brooklyn only to make my way home alone, stopping at a bodega along the way for vitaminwater with last night's makeup still visible around my eyes. There is a small chance that he had some strange belief in serendipity or that he simply forgot to get my number, but I doubt either of those are the case. After a long train ride in fluorescent lighting, I arrived home and peeled off the sweatshirt before I took a hot shower. And instead of throwing it away or putting it in my donation pile, I folded it neatly, the way previous retail experience had taught me. And I placed it in the back of my closet, next to old scrapbooks my aunt had made me when I graduated from college.

These garments that I've collected—mind you, there are only a few—are not special. In fact, few of them are even aesthetically interesting. Yet, they possess a rare quality that borders on metaphysical, housing connections to people and actions that have no other proof of existence. When I get home from late-night ventures, I want to get rid of the clothes. I want to throw them into the clothing abyss and have my wardrobe show no proof of actions that might be deemed questionable by onlookers or my retrospective self. This cultural ritual of hooking up is often quickly followed by a feigned physical and emotional amnesia. And it makes me wonder why do we, why do I, do something that I'm so anxious to forget? I don't want the clothes but I don't want to *not* want the clothes. To throw them away, to donate them would be to leave these blurry nights unexamined. So I keep the sweatshirts and T-shirts and face my growing pile.

Laura Jane Kenny is a fashion writer living in New York.

Meghan O'Rourke

My brother bought this T-shirt at the Saratoga Race Course in 1989. Easy Goer was a three-year-old that year, and he was our favorite horse. We used to go to the Saratoga track every summer with our parents—it was a two-hour drive from the cottage we stayed in. I wanted this shirt, too, but they didn't have my size.

My brother and I were childhood horse-racing junkies. We never went to Disneyland or Great Adventure, but we did go to Aqueduct, Belmont, Saratoga, and Monmouth. Our parents loved racing and they trained us young. My father liked to say I could decode the *Racing Form* before I learned to read, and that is almost the truth.

In the fourth and fifth grades, I could recite, in order, the names of the top-ten-earning thoroughbred sires—the stallions whose offspring won the most races and made the most money. I knew how to look for a cleanly proportioned horse in the paddock. I ate raisin bran in the morning because racehorses ate bran mash. I wanted to be a trainer someday. In the meantime, I kept *Racing Form*–worthy statistics about my imaginary stable's wins.

In 1989 Easy Goer ran the fastest mile that any three-year-old had ever run—quicker even than Secretariat. He was a big handsome chestnut with a bright star on his head. But his story is slightly melancholy.

As a two-year-old, Easy Goer was named champion and became an early favorite for the Kentucky Derby. Horses begin to race when they are two years old, but they often don't come into their own until they are three or four. The Triple Crown, which takes place early in their third year, is a test of stamina and talent.

Leading up to the Derby, Easy Goer looked unbeatable. We thought he would win the Triple Crown, which hadn't been done since 1978. But it rained on Derby day, and Easy Goer's rival, a horse named Sunday Silence, won. Easy Goer didn't like the mud; he came in second, finishing "on class and talent," his jockey said. Then Sunday Silence also beat Easy Goer in the Preakness—by a nose in a photo finish. (Some people think Easy Goer got a bad ride by his jockey.)

At last, in the Belmont Stakes, the third race of the Triple Crown, Easy Goer won by eight lengths. He blew Sunday Silence away. While it would have been thrilling to watch Sunday Silence sweep the Triple Crown, I was excited that Easy Goer came back to beat him in the Belmont, often considered the hardest race in the series because it is the longest.

So when we saw this Easy Goer shirt we wanted it because the red horse was a champion, despite his luck. A week after our trip to Saratoga, Easy Goer beat Sunday Silence at the Travers Stakes, the meet's famous race.

When Easy Goer was eight—still young for a horse—he died of a heart attack. One day, he came running over to his groom in the paddock; moments later he went down on his knees, as the *Los Angeles Times* reported it, and died.

When I was twenty-one, in 1998, I took this shirt from my brother because I hadn't grown much in nine years, and he had. I used to wear it when I went running. It was soft and a little ragged from years of use, and with it on I always felt faster than I really was.

Meghan O'Rourke is a former literary editor at *Slate*, and the author of the memoir *The Long Goodbye* and the poetry collections *Halflife* and *Once*.

Kayla Klepac

It arrived in a small cardboard box on the doorstep of my barely affordable efficiency apartment in Austin, Texas. The boy who sent it had spent a few nights there with me the month prior while visiting from his native France. My ex-boyfriend, who had stuck with me all through college, had just dumped me upon my graduation. I walked off the commencement stage and into the arms of this amorous tourist. He was lonely and I was sad when I pulled him into the stairwell of Speakeasy, a bar on Congress Avenue.

He flew back home but held on to me from across the Atlantic with letters and gifts. The black nightgown was opaque but paper-thin: soft, expensive, and not what I expected from a guy in his early twenties. It was a classy choice, and I like a man with good taste. I liked the anecdote of how his parents had to find discreet ways to get rid of the gerbils he bred as a child; he couldn't bear to keep the male and female gerbils in separate cages. I liked that he gave up a carefree youth to be a successful carpenter and fill his downtown apartment with furniture he made with his own hands; he was missing part of one thumb and I decided there was nothing sexier than a man who knew sacrifice.

I didn't wear the nightgown until I got to France for the kind of clichéd, extended vacation that girlhood dreams are made of. I woke up wearing it in a Paris attic, sun pressing through the slanted skylights. I packed it for our cider-drunk jaunt through England. I wore it in his arms and tried not to admit how cloying they felt. When he was at work, I wore it shamefully late into the day and tried on the role of housewife. I didn't have a car to venture out very far or the language skills to talk to anyone else. I was homesick for whiskey and tacos and Texas men who lost nothing in translation.

In the airport on my way home, he told me he loved me. My name sounded strained and ugly in his accent. He was giving me so much, and all I felt was the fatigue of trying to want it. I was in love with the idea of running away and taking a chance on him, but that was all. It reminded me of when we walked across that bridge in Paris, the one that's covered in locks. It's where lovers take a lock, carve their initials into it, secure it on the metal grating, and then throw the key into the Seine below. When I had to meet his gaze, it felt like opening my eyes underwater in that filthy, romanticized river, feeling around the bottom of the Seine blindly, trying to find the key I had thrown in.

I checked off a life experience. Then I threw away the checklist. I threw away the love notes, but the black nightgown stays buried in one of my dresser drawers. I have a weakness for short and delicate things.

Kayla Klepac is a writer based in Austin, Texas.

Jonathan Levine

Latrell Sprewell was a centerpiece of the 1999 New York Knicks team that miraculously made a run to the NBA Finals. To me, he represented a paradigm of masculinity and a signature type of unjustified, ill-conceived, and immediate rage with which I, as a twenty-three-year-old Jewish kid from the Upper East Side, completely identified. In those days Sprewell would hurtle down the court with no plan whatsoever, then just take it to the hole or hoist up a shot that would make his coach cringe. And if that coach didn't like it, Spree, as he was called, just might choke the motherfucker.

Spree would often take over games because he didn't know any better. This almost willful ignorance, this incomparable ability to tune out the haters, put his head down, and just drive, actually kinda worked. The Knicks, who barely made the playoffs in 1999 with a 28–23 record, proceeded to become the first eighth-seeded team to get to the NBA Finals, blowing right by anyone who told them they weren't good enough. It was around this time that I bought Spree's number eight Knicks jersey in the blue-and-orange away colors.

I got it at Gerry Cosby. It fit snug. And wearing it was an act of embracing my inner Spree: the guy who would defy you by hoisting up a thirty-foot jumper, or choke you for no apparent reason. I wasn't very good at basketball—some might say I was awful—and I have long suffered from a debilitating neck injury that makes it difficult to run or jump. But I identified with Spree nonetheless.

I wore the jersey in my Brown University thesis film, which I directed and in which I was also charged with the unfortunate duty of acting. I liked the finished product and I liked the way I looked in the Spree jersey, so I wore it on the first day of my next film in film school, and the next. It became something of a good luck charm, as well as a hidden mission statement. See, as I got older, any bluster Sprewell and I shared dissipated with each passing year. The notion that I would identify with a six-foot-five, cornrowed two-guard actually ended up seeming pretty ridiculous. But wearing this jersey signaled that it was still within me, somewhere. That if you pushed me far enough, I just might choke you out. Metaphorically.

The jersey was lucky until it wasn't. I remember wearing it on one particularly ignominious professional occasion and cursing Spree as I slunk home in defeat, vowing never to wear it again. I guess the jersey's luck had run out. The Knicks' luck ran out, too. In 1999, when they finally arrived at the NBA Finals, the San Antonio Spurs defeated them in five games. The Spurs were bigger and better, and they made the Knicks look every bit the slightly above-average team we all feared they might be. They haven't gotten anywhere close to the Finals since.

So I guess the whole "lucky item of clothing thing" is kinda silly. I liked this jersey because of the way it made me feel and because of what it represented, not because it had any magical powers. I'm sure Spree didn't believe in luck. He didn't believe in shit, except himself, even when he had absolutely no business believing in himself. And a lot of the time that worked. Maybe that's what some mistake for luck. I don't really know.

I do know that I never could bring myself to toss the Spree jersey. I still wear it, but most often when I'm doing laundry or when I have to dig particularly deep in my clothing rotation. And sometimes when I rock it—as I'm gingerly placing a dryer sheet atop a pile of dirty laundry in my Los Angeles apartment complex, so far from New York and from the person I was when I bought it—I remember that remarkable Knicks team. And for a fleeting moment, I feel like anything is possible.

Jonathan Levine is a film director and screenwriter whose films include *Warm Bodies*, *50/50*, and *The Wackness*.

Yael Meridan Schori

I was eighteen when I was drafted into the Israeli army, and I was looking for excitement. Somehow, I convinced my superior in the commando unit that I needed to take the men's parachute course. I wiggled my way into the course because he thought I was young and cute and that it would be good for morale.

At that time women in the army didn't fight. They were meant to relieve men from secretarial work, act as social workers, and fold parachutes. Today women are much more active, but from 1970 to 1972 that wasn't the case. Every time the unit went parachuting, I'd join them, but I'd never parachute during a mission, or over enemy lines.

Whenever we'd jump during training, I'd go first. I'd wait by the open door of the airplane and my commander would say, "If she's brave enough to jump, then any man can jump."

Every course had one night jump, so we'd parachute in pitch black. My boyfriend at the time, who was in the same unit, would wait for me on the ground. Before every jump, they'd send out a dummy to test the wind conditions. Since I was always first, I'd jump after the dummy. One night, they kept sending out one dummy after another because their parachutes did not open. By the time I jumped, my boyfriend was hysterical. He was certain that my parachute had malfunctioned.

I'd grown up as a tomboy and had this "everything you can do, I can do better" kind of attitude. In order to take the paratrooper course, your parents had to sign a permission form, and my father refused: "There's no way I'm signing this form. I'm not letting you do this." I told him that if he didn't sign, I'd falsify his signature. As a conscientious attorney, he immediately signed. They didn't even have parachuting clothes that fit me, so they had to order special paratrooper boots in my size.

One weekend when I was visiting my boyfriend, he and I were practicing our paratrooper rolls on the sand dunes; when you land, you have to roll onto your shoulder to divide the impact on your whole body. His platoon saw somebody rolling down the dunes but didn't know who it was—they were positive we were infiltrators and their guns were drawn, ready to shoot. We sat down and lit a cigarette (we were still smoking back then), and the soldiers realized that we couldn't be the enemy since we were sitting down and smoking. So they looked around to see who was missing, and realized it was the two of us.

I was the first female in our commando unit to parachute. Over two years I parachuted fourteen times. There's a photo of me in the Israeli newspaper *Maariv* after one of those jumps.

When I completed the course, I received a pin with parachute wings on a blue vinyl background. I wore it on the front left side of my uniform, alongside the other pin of my commando unit, and right above my heart, to show that I had earned my wings as a paratrooper.

—AS TOLD TO EMILY SPIVACK

Yael Meridan Schori served in the Israeli Army from 1970 to 1972 and then became a flight attendant. She immigrated to the U.S. in 1980 and is the chairwoman of Art Resources Transfer in New York.

Albert Maysles

My first venture abroad was in 1955. I borrowed a movie camera from CBS and went to Russia to make a film about mental hospitals. Through film, my intention was to represent ordinary people and use visual imagery to establish a bond between Americans and Russians.

I like to pick up clothing when I'm in a foreign country. At the time, a very commonly worn quilted jacket known as a *fufaika* identified one as a Russian peasant. I wanted one, but it wasn't something you could buy in Moscow. People didn't wear them in the city. You had to go outside of the city to find one. I don't know why; maybe the government didn't want people from abroad to associate Russia with peasants.

At the time foreigners were not supposed to go outside of the cities, but I did. I took the train to see what it was like beyond Moscow. And during that trip, I found my fufaika. I was drawn to it; it symbolized the working class of Russia, and it was forbidden.

I began wearing the jacket when I returned to New York City. I put a lot of wear into it. Somewhere there's a photo of me and my brother riding around on motorcycles and I'm wearing that jacket.

Years later, a Russian friend of mine, Mikhail Baryshnikov, came over to my apartment at the Dakota. I don't know what brought me to do it, but I opened my closet and showed him my fufaika, and when I did, it brought tears to his eyes.

—AS TOLD TO EMILY SPIVACK

Albert Maysles is a documentarian whose films include *Salesman*, *Gimme Shelter*, and *Grey Gardens*.

Paola Antonelli

I was scared walking to school every morning. To get there, I had to pass through the area that separated the neo-fascist extremists that hung out in Piazza San Babila, and the leftist group that congregated at the Leonardo da Vinci science high school, which was right next door to my school.

I went to the Collegio delle Fanciulle, which means "damsels' college." (They've since changed the name to Liceo Emanuela Setti Carraro, dedicated to General Dalla Chiesa's wife, who was killed with him by the mafia in 1982.) The school was founded by Napoleon for his generals' daughters when he conquered Italy. It's a beautiful place with a great garden and frescos.

Across our wall, topped by broken glass and barbed wire, the leftist guys who had occupied the da Vinci high school would come on the megaphone, luring us out to the garden saying, "Fanciulle, come out and play!"

Frequently we would have bomb threats during school and class would be disrupted, so it was easy to sneak out. I told my friends, "I can't stay in this beautiful place while it feels like the whole world is exploding around us." With me as the ringleader, four of us—the damsels—went over to the da Vinci high school to see what it was all about. They showed us around; they were all camping there, writing on the wall and just doing their political activism thing, waiting to clash with the Sanbabilini.

You could tell they were on the left because they wore peacoats and jeans and would carry messenger bags made of green military fabric. Their statement was one of rejecting fashion, but in truth, they were very stylized, too.

The Sanbabilini scared me much more than the extremists on the left. They were usually gun-toting neo-fascists from wealthy Milanese families who shared responsibility for much of the violence around Italy at that time.

The Sanbabilini had a distinctive look: they dressed elegantly in fitted shirts, trench coats, penny loafers—or Gucci loafers for the girls—and Ray-Ban Aviator sunglasses. Their look was very proper and posh.

Sometime in the late 1970s, during this time of upheaval, my father came home from his first trip to the United States with a pair of Ray-Ban Aviators he'd bought for me. He had not thought of the political implications; he had just wanted a gift that embodied "America." Even though it was only a pair of sunglasses, it was like holding a bomb in my hands. I couldn't wear them.

Along the way, the first pair of Aviators disappeared, and I decided to buy myself another pair. They never looked good on me, but it was a sort of exorcism. Even then, years later, it felt almost like they were burning in my hands; they transport me to a moment that was formative, but one that I also want to forget.

I compare notes with friends who grew up in Israel or Beirut, for example, and I realize we all went through something similar—living despite the bombs going off, despite the fact that it was almost a war zone. Little details, like scents or sounds or a piece of clothing bring back the violence, and that's what these Aviators do for me.

—AS TOLD TO EMILY SPIVACK

Paola Antonelli is senior curator in the Department of Architecture and Design and director of research and development at the Museum of Modern Art.

Catherine Pierce

If the skirt were a person, it would have been pleasant but unflappable. It would have worn horn-rim glasses and bestowed smiles on only the most intelligent and outcast students. It would have used words like "consequentially" and "reprimand." It would, I hoped, convince my students that I was some sort of authority figure, and it would also, I hoped even more, convince me. The thought of teaching freshman composition made me nauseated. As a freshman myself, I'd imagined my professors materializing in the classroom as the first students entered, and then vanishing into mist—*poof!*—when the hour and ten minutes were up. It had never occurred to me that they might be human.

In that fall of 2001 I was an MFA student entering my first semester of teaching. One week earlier the country had changed permanently. These days, everyone froze and watched, not breathing, each time a plane floated by. Afternoons were pocked with moments of silence. The bright blue of Ohio fall had taken on a sinister cast as we waited for whatever was coming next. In the midst of this, I went to the mall and spent far more money than I should have, given my grad student stipend, on an elegant checked pencil skirt from Ann Taylor. Even though I looked no older than the eighteen- and nineteen-year-olds I'd be teaching, wearing the skirt, I felt older than twenty-three. And I felt, at least a little bit, like the world, which was suddenly splintering, could be whipped back into shape.

I wore the skirt with a fitted black sweater and black shoes. In retrospect, the skirt should never have been worn with black, and the shoes I'd purchased were absurd—my twenty-three-year-old self's idea of "formal"—clunky, rubber-soled Mary Janes that could have doubled as gardening shoes. But I liked the ensemble. Wearing that pencil skirt and that fitted top, I felt taller, in charge, a little uncomfortable in a way that kept me on my toes. And when I walked into my classroom that first day and saw my class staring back at me (four girls and twenty guys), I was grateful for the drawing-in and shoring-up of those clothes. We did our introductions. I learned that one of the men was forty-two; he spent the day (and the semester) leering at the four young women. One of the men was an ex-Marine and Harley enthusiast, and talked about nothing else. One man was from Saudi Arabia and talked about how uncomfortable he was in the States these days, how afraid he was of his family being harassed. One of the girls said she was homesick. One of the guys had been in Manhattan when the towers fell.

I didn't know what to say to any of them. I was homesick, too, and terrified of being called a fraud. The blue sky outside the window hummed with invisible threats. We were all ill at ease and surrounded by a city that was newly unfamiliar. But my clothes felt like a uniform, something you put on to do a job. I felt my body gathered in by the snug skirt, the black sweater, and heard myself beginning sentences without knowing where they'd end, just trusting they'd land somewhere that made sense. Miraculously, most of the time they did.

When the class time was up that first day, I told the students what their homework was for the next meeting, and they wrote it down. When I said, "See you on Thursday," a few of them said it back. They left while I pretended to pack up. I stood in the empty classroom for a minute, quietly surging with the illusion of my authority. Then I stepped into the hallway and felt myself vanish back into who I was—someone human, someone buffeted by the dark new world.

Catherine Pierce is a poet, English professor, and the author of *The Girls of Peculiar* and *Famous Last Words*.

April Bloomfield

I'm from England, and I always wanted to move to America. I grew up watching *The Goonies* and tons of American police shows, and my dream was to join the New York Police Department.

Instead of joining the NYPD, I wound up becoming a chef. I got this great opportunity to come to New York to cook and open my first restaurant, a gastro-pub called The Spotted Pig, with my business partner, Ken Friedman. I really didn't know what to expect when I got to New York, but it just so happens that The Spotted Pig was successful, for which I am humbly grateful.

I came here on an O-1 visa, and after three years I had to apply for a green card. I went through the process, which was super exciting, and I promised myself that I would do something very American when I got my green card, a celebratory event for me and nobody else.

The day I received my green card, I knew I wanted to treat myself to a pair of Converse. After all, what's more American than Converse? I went to David Z on 14th Street and took a long time choosing the right style, a pair of high tops that fit me perfectly and were very comfortable. I popped my Converse cherry on that day. I've probably gone through fifteen pairs since then; I wear them until they drop off my feet or they walk off on their own.

My first pair of Converse, and every pair since, has been a way to embrace my time here. Since I moved to America, I've met amazing people, eaten the most delicious food in the world, and welcomed how free and easy it is. It's been a crazy trip, a crazy dream.

—AS TOLD TO EMILY SPIVACK

April Bloomfield is the executive chef and co-owner of The Spotted Pig, The Breslin Bar & Dining Room, The John Dory Oyster Bar, and Salvation Taco, in New York City, as well as Tosca Cafe in San Francisco. She is also the author of a cookbook, *A Girl and Her Pig*.

Brian Dwyer

I had been walking past an airbrush artist at the Market East Station in Philadelphia for two years on my way to my job at Trader Joe's, and I always thought his joker faces and yin-yang designs were pretty good. One day I asked him if he could make a T-shirt with a pizza that said "Endless Joy." I had him make two—for me and for one of my dearest pizza brothers, Chris. Chris and I shared a studio together, and we'd begun working on a music project we called Endless Joy. I'd recently left my band after five years and was figuring out what my next project might be. That spring Chris and I discovered a shared love for pizza. I'd bring strange posters, or little toys, or pizza boxes with drawings on them into the studio and that began my pizza collection. But the T-shirt was the first thing I got in earnest to express my love for pizza.

As the collection in my studio grew, I began looking at pizza in a different way, as a kind of vehicle for creativity. And thus started the strange journey of seeing life through a lens of pizza.

One day I went into the studio and said to Chris, "You know what would be really fun? If we curated an art show where everybody contributed work about pizza." It was an idea that I took way too seriously. Plus, I'd never curated an art show before. We billed it as Philadelphia's first pizza-centric art show, and at the opening over four hundred people showed up, ages five to ninety. It was a huge success, with everyone celebrating life and pizza.

I woke up the next morning completely changed, and thought, "Why have I never been to a pizza shop that was aware of the culture of pizza—not just the food—but the feeling of community that comes from eating pizza?" That was the birth of my idea for Pizza Brain.

The next summer, as the project started gaining momentum and I was building Pizza Brain, I thought it'd be funny if, as part of the restaurant, we had the largest collection of pizza-related ephemera in Pennsylvania, or on the East Coast. My partner Mike and I did some extensive research on Google to see who was the Guinness record holder and nothing came up. Once I realized no one was the record holder, I applied for the paperwork, filled out the forms, and organized another pop-up gallery two doors down from the original art show to display this quickly amassing pizza-related collection.

We picked up the Guinness Book of World Records rep from the train station. She was wearing her Guinness one-piece uniform and was very professional. She walked through the space and counted, taking into consideration the various Guinness regulations, and with 561 items we got the record right there in front of the neighborhood for the world's first pizza museum.

Two and a half years later, the pizza collection has grown into the thousands. Because the pizza shop is here to stay, I've got a permanent home for this collection, a temple for people to really celebrate it.

I've worn this T-shirt everywhere: from the Hoover Dam to the walls of Quebec City, from the Pacific Coast Highway to New Jersey and back. I wear it when I'm feeling bummed and I know it's time to get pumped. In fact, I probably wear it once a week, especially if I'm working in the pizza shop. It all started with this shirt. It's very sentimental, the perfect representation of how I feel about pizza—it's endless joy.

—AS TOLD TO EMILY SPIVACK

Brian Dwyer is a co-owner of the Pizza Brain pizzeria and museum in Philadelphia.

Debbie Millman

I don't remember her name, but I remember how she smelled: it was a heady mix of baby powder and wildflowers with a sliver of orange. I had never experienced anything like it before. It was twenty-five years ago and I'd just met her; she was the prospective client in a pitch for a graphic design project. She was slender and elegant, with thin arms and a long neck. As an awkward, chubby, twenty-something New Yorker, I nearly always felt ashamed in the presence of women who projected her kind of confidence, but it didn't stop me from trying to emulate them. When I commented on her perfume and asked what it was, she said something that sounded like Fabergé, but I knew it wasn't Fabergé. I was familiar with what Fabergé smelled like: all the girls wore it in high school. This was not that fragrance, not by a long shot.

We didn't win the project, but I couldn't stop thinking about that perfume! I went searching at Macy's, and tried Bloomingdale's and Loehmann's to no avail. I made my way over to Saks Fifth Avenue, but felt shabby and intimidated by the sophisticated salesladies and was afraid to ask for help. I poked around the cosmetics counters, and when one of the makeup artists asked if I wanted a makeover, I shook my head no. When she asked if she could help me with anything, I cleared my throat and asked if she had ever heard of a citrusy smelling fragrance with a name like Fabergé. She thought for a minute and then her face lit up. She thought I might be talking about Faubourg, a new fragrance by Hermés. I asked her which counter might have it. She frowned and indicated that they didn't sell the fragrance at Saks, but I could get it at the Hermés boutique on Madison Avenue just a few blocks away.

I nearly ran to the store. When I got there, a man in a uniform opened the door for me and I entered the most elegantly expensive environment I had ever been in. Two hundred dollar scarves and ten thousand dollar bags were neatly arranged on glass counters, shiny leather saddles hung on the walls, and everyone browsing looked very, very rich, except for me. I found Faubourg and gulped when the saleslady stated the price. I wondered whether a bottle of perfume could be worth so much, and meekly asked if I could try it. I swooned as soon as the spray hit my skin and handed over my credit card.

Every couple of months I took the E train to 53rd Street and walked to Hermés for a refill, but I couldn't afford to buy anything else. That changed when I visited the store in July 1990. A saleslady beckoned me closer and whispered, "We are having a sale on select items upstairs."

Even with the markdowns, I couldn't afford anything. And then I saw the most beautiful coat. It was the softest, most luxurious, ultra-bright lemony-yellow cashmere coat ever made. It had big, floppy lapels and a belt that cinched at the waist. I was certain it would cost thousands of dollars. And it did: $2,200. But the original price was crossed out! It was now $400.

I calculated what the expense would mean to my budget. Undeterred, I tried the coat on. It was at least one size too big. None of this mattered to me. I felt glamorous and beautiful. As the clerk wrapped up the coat in the biggest orange box I had ever seen, I knew this wasn't a mistake. I would wear this coat *forever*.

And wear it I did! I wore it every day from September until March. I wore it to work, I wore it every weekend, I wore it on vacation in Vermont, and I wore it traveling to the West Coast. The only time I wished for a warmer coat was en route to a client's office on Fifth Avenue one blustery subzero February afternoon. I was chewing a large piece of purple bubble gum and realized I'd have to get rid of it before my meeting. It was so cold I didn't want to take my gloves off to take the gum out of my mouth. Perhaps the temperature affected my judgment, or perhaps I was lazy, but suddenly I did something I had never, ever done before: I raised my chin, puckered up my lips, and let my gum fly. As it descended onto the sidewalk, I saw that a man walking toward me was about to collide with the arc of its fall. I made eye contact with him as the sticky mass fell at his feet. Horrified, I instantly realized I was face-to-face with Woody Allen. Mercifully, he sidestepped the gum. But his outrage was palpable. He shook his head in disgust and passed me by. I was too embarrassed and frightened to even say I was sorry.

Two days later I went out with my friend Ellen. She had snagged a reservation at the newly reopened Le Cirque and we got all dolled up for the occasion. I, of course, wore my yellow coat. We were seated between the coat check and the front door, and since New York City was still in a deep freeze, I decided to keep my coat wrapped around me.

Then I saw him. He was approaching the coat check with his wife, fumbling for his ticket. Wildly, I looked around for a place to hide. Ellen asked me if I was okay and I hissed, *no*. I motioned with my eyes. Ellen squealed in delight, and he looked over at us. Once again, in the span of forty-eight hours, I was face-to-face with Woody Allen.

Our eyes locked and I saw him recognize my unmistakable ultra-bright yellow coat and the same frightened face. He grimaced. "You!" he said, as his wife pulled on his arm. I felt myself turn white and then red, as everyone turned to stare.

Two and a half decades later, I still have my beloved coat. It's lost its belt and much of its lemony sheen, and it hasn't left its special place in my closet in a long time. Maybe I'll wear it again one day. As Woody Allen famously said, "Eternal nothingness is fine if you happen to be dressed for it." I'll remind him of that if I ever bump into him again.

Debbie Millman is a writer, educator, artist, and designer.

Harvey

I was the wacky morning DJ at a Philadelphia radio station for fourteen years, starting in 1977. When I got fired, it was the single most devastating event of my life. It's not an exaggeration; I've lost both parents. I've been divorced. I've been through some stuff and nothing has even come close to what I felt after I was fired.

Around that time I got a call from a production assistant who'd been a fan of my radio show. "We've got a messy kids game show for Nickelodeon," she tells me, "and they need an announcer. Interested?" I was out of work so I said sure. I did some kind of audition, sent them a cassette tape demo, and got cast as the off-camera announcer for *Double Dare*.

The show grew quickly, and after the first sixty-five episodes the executive producers discovered that I had a performance background. My role morphed from an off-screen voice to the goofy sidekick of host Marc Summers. *The Tonight Show* was still on, so Johnny Carson and Ed McMahon were our models. Marc and I would banter back and forth, and sometimes I'd demonstrate stunts for the physical challenge part of the game show. They'd often dress me up—a clown, baseball player, boxer, ballerina, Tarzan, gorilla, Santa Claus. It was always a delightful surprise when the wardrobe person would say, "I need to measure you for your ape costume." I got to play the crafty fool, and they gave me a lot of latitude.

A couple of seasons in, we started doing live versions of *Double Dare*, including a shopping mall tour. Malls were horrible places to play because the acoustics are too echoey and nobody pays attention—they didn't come to see you. But because the show was increasingly popular, we went on an arena tour and would fill twenty-thousand-seat halls, places that bands would play. For a guy who from seventh grade on wanted to be a rock star, hosting a show in front of a crowd of twenty thousand kids who were screaming, "Pick me! Put a pie in my face!" was like a dream come true, even if those kids

were a little younger than what I'd originally had in mind.

While we'd begun shooting *Double Dare* in Philadelphia, for the last two or three years we shot it at Universal Studios in Florida, which was just like the movie sets I remembered seeing as a kid. Every morning I'd drive past the guard shack, and the guard would recognize me, say "Good morning, Harvey," and wave me through. I would pull into my parking space with my name on it and go into my dressing room with my name on it. Those were the moments that you know are not going to last forever, so you try to take everything in.

I really knew we'd made it when I heard we were going to be parodied in *Mad* magazine. I'd read the magazine as a kid and they'd always done parodies of all the big movies and TV shows. I couldn't believe they were doing *Double Dare*. Because I was the sidekick, I hoped they'd do at least one caricature of me in one panel, but they actually wound up featuring me prominently throughout the whole parody. They called the show "Double Damp," Marc was "Muck Slummers" and I was "Hardly." I've got a framed copy on my wall because it was one of the showbiz pinnacles for me—it was beyond words.

The show went into syndication on the Fox network, which was a new broadcast network at that point. They only had programming on Saturday nights for three shows—*Married with Children, The Tracey Ullman Show,* and *Family Double Dare. Family Double Dare* was a grown-up version of the show we'd been doing, where instead of teams of just kids, they included two parents and two kids. Since it was nighttime, the network decided to make it spiffy. They changed the set, took us out of our jeans and T-shirts, and put Marc in a tuxedo and me in a red tails tuxedo. We could sense the pressure coming from the new network. I had to prove my value again, in my tuxedo, to this network and to people in Los

Angeles, whom I never saw because they watched the show getting taped via satellite.

We had shot sixteen episodes in New York at this point, and I wore my red tuxedo on every episode. The show got renewed for another season, and we were thrilled, especially considering the pressure we'd initially felt. Hotel rooms were reserved at the Pierre for the crew for the length of time it would take to shoot another sixteen episodes. They'd pulled the sets and costumes, including my tuxedo, out of the warehouse and assembled everything in the studio.

At the end of the first day of rehearsal, the executive producer gathered us around and said, "Well, I have some interesting news for you folks. *Family Double Dare* has just been canceled." As we struggled to digest what that meant, he came over and asked me if I liked my red tails tuxedo. By then, I'd grown to love it. "It's yours then. Just take it," he told me. It was my parting gift for the whole deal.

—AS TOLD TO EMILY SPIVACK

Harvey was a television and radio personality, and the announcer for *Double Dare*.
He is now a handyman who runs his own business.

Susan Orlean

I've always wanted to find the perfect uniform. I often think I've found it, and I will buy it in multiple quantities. I'm convinced that I'll wear it forever, and that it's the perfect representation of my personal style. Then the inevitable always occurs: I put on that perfect thing, look in the mirror, and wonder, "Oy, what was I thinking?" It's a little like waking up one day and—thankfully this hasn't happened to me!—looking at your husband and thinking, "Oh my God, I'm in the wrong relationship." Every time I fell in love with one of these uniforms, I never believed that the feeling would pass.

This happened with a certain style of pants made by a store in New York called Reminiscence. With its side zipper and very pegged ankle, I thought they were the perfect pair of pants, so I bought a million pairs of the same cut in corduroy, cotton, and stripes. One day, though, I put them on and they just looked awful on me. That was the end of those pants.

The next iteration of this uniform fixation was an outfit made by Dosa—a long button-down shirtdress worn over pants. I thought, "I have found it. This is me. I am at peace now." I bought several sets, which was a big investment because their clothes are not cheap. During a trip to Bangkok, I even took the outfit to one of those tailors who copies whatever you bring them in about five minutes and had more made. I wore this outfit on my first book tour in 1989, day after day. I thought I would grow old in it. About two years after I had invested most of my disposable income in this particular assemblage, the veil dropped from my eyes.

It's a temporary delusion that comes over me with regularity—a belief that by wearing this perfect thing, I will look right and feel good no matter what. Like, "How did I not know that I'm an agnès b. T-shirt and denim skirt kind of person? Now, I'm going to order ten of each and I never have to buy clothes again." When I'm in it, I totally believe I have found my look, my personal style. It's cultish and my own particular mania. Each time I start over again, I think, "those were false gods— I have now found the true God." I even observe myself doing it. I understand that fashion, by definition, is a changing thing, and so is one's body. I try to talk myself out of my own crazy conviction that I've finally solved the puzzle—and yet I can't do it.

I guess it's probably safer to be this way about clothing than men or religion or something that could be really dangerous. I'm quite pragmatic about other choices in my life, but with clothing I'm a romantic—I abandon myself completely and the practical side gets trumped. I become a zealot.

—AS TOLD TO EMILY SPIVACK

Susan Orlean is a staff writer for the *New Yorker*.

Stephen Elliott

I've had this backpack for seven years. I got it while on a shopping spree at the Nike employee store. How I got a shopping spree at the Nike employee store is another story, one I don't quite understand myself, but everybody I knew got a free pair of shoes that week.

The thing about the bag is that it was never released. People don't believe it's Nike until I show them the swoosh just inside the leather strap. I say it's a prototype, which is not exactly accurate. There were a couple of them at the employee store and that was it. Price tag: $200. More than I would ever pay for a fashion accessory, or it was. (I recently bought a scooter.)

This bag falls apart and so I have to take it to the shoe repair. Maybe that's why the bag was never released. I have to get it stitched a couple times a year. I had a canvas liner installed inside the bag but soon the bag will be too busted to contain it.

Still, I keep fixing it because every week someone comments on it and I've never had something like that before and I probably won't again. I mean, no one has ever commented on my shirt or my pants or my shoes. I don't have much style. I still wear white T-shirts and blue jeans almost every day, like I did in grammar school. Though maybe that will change as well. (I've recently been wearing grayish and dark blue T-shirts.)

I didn't realize this bag was so stylish, though now it seems obvious. It takes me a while to recognize beauty; that's why, as a writer, I edit so compulsively.

Now I'm not sure what to do. I've spent more than $200 on this free thing. The bag needs to be retired, or undergo a severe restitching. I can't afford to lose my keys and wallet. I shouldn't use the bag for heavy things, like my computer and hard drives, but I do. Because I don't have another one.

Stephen Elliott is a filmmaker and author of The Adderall Diaries, Happy Baby, *and* A Life Without Consequences. *He also founded the online literary website* The Rumpus.

Emily Spivack

Like always, I was walking down Rehoboth Avenue with my grandmother. We went past Dolle's Salt Water Taffy, Thrasher's French Fries, Summer Winds T-shirt Shop, and the place where you could dress up in prairie costumes and get your sepia-toned photo taken—honky-tonk shops that line the main drag and lead to the boardwalk, stores I'd seen since I was wheeled down the avenue in a stroller.

The sun was bright and I wore conspicuously oversized sunglasses. I could feel the heat on my pink, freckled shoulders as I hobbled along on flip-flops that had just broken. It was my grandmother who insisted we stop into South Moon Under for a new pair. She perused the aisles, her bosom well contained beneath her grandma bathing suit and netted cover-up. "What about these?" she asked, gesturing with tanned, leathery arms at the pegs full of options: magenta, teal, polka-dotted, striped. Instead, I chose a simple black sturdy pair by Flojo, size 8. My grandmother paid, I slipped on the thongs—as my grandmother called them—and we were on our way. As we walked back to my family's red umbrella on the beach, I could hear the Flojos flopping against the wooden boardwalk planks.

That was 1997 but I'm still wearing that pair of Flojos. And since then, flip-flop fashion has become ubiquitous. They've spread beyond the summer months, becoming acceptable footwear with suits and cocktail dresses as well as bathing suits and shorts. Expensive name brands have emerged, with bejeweled versions fetching four figures. Girls wear gold flip-flop charm necklaces. But for as long as I can remember, I've had exactly one simple pair.

"Who has flip-flops for sixteen years?" my sister, Lauren, asked on a recent family beach vacation. She told me she cycles through a couple pairs every year. They break, they wear out, they get left behind.

Mine didn't. You could chalk up part of that time to a stylistic phase, several years long, during which I only wore boots and hulking, multi-inch platform shoes, the footwear component of a nun-like style. I liked being covered up year-round, even if it meant tights, twenty-hole lace-ups, and layers of crinoline under a full skirt in New York City's thickest August humidity. During that stretch, I wouldn't even consider wearing sandals, and my flip-flops emerged from my closet for very occasional pool or beachside use.

And yet, I kept them. Because I hang on to stuff. Like the rest of my belongings, these flip-flops have traveled with me from college to real life, from apartment to apartment, from Wilmington to Providence to New York to Philadelphia, and finally back to New York. I've got concert T-shirts from seventh grade, socks from summer camp, long flowing dresses from high school. I guess I find comfort in these things.

Through years of inadvertent preservation, these slip-ons have done some globetrotting. They've been in every hotel room where I wanted something between me and the grungy carpet; on every beach, from Fire Island to Fenwick Island, from Tulum to Turks and Caicos; in grimy hostel bathrooms on European backpacking trips. It's like I find them waiting for me in my suitcase without realizing I've even packed them.

But mostly these Flojos wind up accompanying me on mundane activities, like sorting delicates at the laundromat, mailing the rent check, or stocking up on apple cider donuts at the farmers market. That's how, over time, these flip-flops—plain, pulled from a rack without a thought, manufactured to be disposable but apparently indestructible—have become such a lasting fixture in my life. Precisely, perhaps, because they are so ordinary: you don't even notice them casually accumulating the years, like the shops along Rehoboth Avenue, like grandmothers, like everything.

Emily Spivack created *Worn Stories*.

Piper Kerman

I have loved vintage clothing since I was in high school, thrifting the racks or raiding my grandparents' attics and closets. I attended a lot of morning college classes clad in old men's pajamas. Skinny-lapeled men's suit jackets over miniskirts were a favorite in my twenties. I've worn crepe dresses from the thirties and forties to friends' weddings, and when I was getting married I found my fiancé the white silk suit of a dead Chinese diplomat to wear on the big day (I got one of the diplomat's wife's cheongsams for me).

In some instances I'm less inclined to wear vintage. During my late twenties, when I was caught in a criminal case, I wore my most sober gray and brown pantsuits to the federal court arraignments and plea negotiations in Chicago. When you're appearing on the docket, believe me, you wish you could disappear into the woodwork of the courtroom.

However, when I went to what I thought was my final court appearance, my sentencing, camouflage was not an option. I had taken a plea deal—95 percent of criminal defendants do. As your case wends through the system, you barely speak in court; the prosecutor and defense attorney do most of the talking. Unlike 80 percent of criminal defendants, I could afford to hire a lawyer, and I was lucky that he was a very good and experienced one. He had advocated long and hard with the prosecutor on my behalf, and then the day came where his work and my case would be decided by the judge, a Reagan appointee to the federal bench.

Most criminal defendants wear whatever they are given by their attorney or family to their sentencing; a lot of people are too poor to afford bail, and so they have been wearing jailhouse orange for many months before ever getting their day in court. I was much more fortunate; when I flew to Chicago to be sentenced to prison, I had three choices of court attire in my suitcase. A cadet-blue pantsuit, a very severe navy coatdress, and a wild card I had packed at the last minute: a vintage fifties pencil-skirt suit I had bought on eBay, in a coffee and cream tweed with a subtle sky blue check. It looked like something a Hitchcock heroine would have worn.

"That's the one," said my lawyer, pointing to the skirt suit. "We want the judge to be reminded of his own daughter or niece or neighbor when he looks at you."

For someone standing for judgment, the importance of being seen as a complete human being, someone who is more than just the contents of the file folders that rest on the bench in front of His or Her Honor, cannot be overstated. To enter the courtroom ready for whatever would happen, I wanted to be dressed to represent *me*, which was much more than a few months of my life ten years past. The eBay suit worked as a counterbalance to my decade-old neck tattoo (which would serve me so well months later in prison), two visual signals on the opposite sides of the scales of justice on that day.

Piper Kerman is the author of the memoir *Orange Is the New Black: My Year in a Women's Prison*, which was adapted into an original television series for Netflix.

Sabrina Gschwandtner

Bathrobes are transitional. You put them on temporarily, between waking and eating breakfast, showering and dressing, undressing and sleeping.

I've worn this bathrobe for the past ten years, during countless daily transitions and through major turning points in my adult life.

I started wearing it as a guest at my boyfriend's apartment. He wanted me to feel comfortable, so he offered me a choice between two robes: this cotton, Kimono-style robe with a blue and white pattern and billowing sleeves or a tan one that's monogrammed with his four initials. I wasn't particularly drawn to either one, so I chose unmonogrammed because it seemed more neutral.

When we moved in together, the robe was unpacked and moved to my side of the closet. That's when I started thinking of it as mine, and not a borrowed item.

I wore my robe less often after we got married. I guess my sense of modesty waned.

When I got pregnant, I wore it a lot. It was the only garment that comfortingly fit during my entire forty-two week pregnancy.

On summer nights I would put it on and turn sideways in front of our full-length mirror, feeling around for a bump. By late winter, after rejecting other clothes for being small, impractical, or uncomfortable, I would put on the bathrobe and lie down, bypassing the mirror altogether.

I brought the bathrobe to the hospital when I gave birth. I packed enough clothes to live there for a month, but the robe is the only thing I remember wearing. I can't look at it now without flashing back to one particular hour of my twenty-six hour labor, when I put on the bathrobe and announced to my nurse Bianca, "We have to get out of here!" We left my husband, mother, and doula in birthing room two and crossed the hall to room five, which was empty and had a better view. There I began walking in circles around the room, which birthing books call "a spontaneous ritual," an activity women come up with in the moment to deal with labor pain. I carefully timed each step so that my circle would last the length of a contraction. I remember starting each new circle by the window thinking, I just have to make it back to the window again….

I wore the robe so much during the first few months of my son's life that I'm sure he thought it was my skin. He was at risk of jaundice when he was born, so I was advised to breastfeed him hourly. I didn't have time to do anything but breastfeed and sleep, so instead of changing my clothes I just wore the robe around the clock, mostly unaware of whether it was day or night. I would pull open the bathrobe and nurse while my husband spoon-fed me chicken salad and fruit, trying not to spill any of it on our kid's head.

Gradually my days and nights separated again, and now the bathrobe is my morning uniform. I pull it on at five o'clock in the morning when my son wakes up and he uses it as a communication system during the early morning hours before his first nap. He tugs on the hemline and looks at me pleadingly when he wants to be lifted up. He reaches for the robe at my knees when he wants me to help him walk. And he grabs it and rolls over onto his back when he's feeling tired. I'd like to say that after I put him down to nap in his crib I disrobe, shower, and get dressed for the day, but usually I fall back into bed and wake up an hour later with the robe twisted around me.

Sabrina Gschwandtner is an artist living in Brooklyn.

Dorothy Finger

Life was very good until September 1, 1939. I was an only child, and my parents had a small department store in Chodorow, a part of Poland that is now in Ukraine. They called us bourgeois, but we weren't wealthy. We were upper middle-class Jews. When the bombing started we were occupied by the Russian army. Before we went into hiding, and before the Russian army put a lock on the department store and said it belonged to the people, my parents managed to get a few things out. They gave some of their belongings to gentile families for safekeeping.

We were in hiding in a barn for a while. I lived in three ghettos. My father was the first one killed. He was almost beaten to death and then sent to an extermination camp. Later, my mother was shot. I was sent to a labor camp, where we were made to build roads. I had to carry buckets of stones and pour tar over them. I was beaten by the Nazis. It was slave labor.

July 27, 1943, is the day I went into the forest. They started shooting in the labor camp. We heard machine guns and we ran. Somehow I managed to get under the electrified wire at the edge of the camp; some people were electrocuted. The camp was very close to a forest and I ran into it with my aunt and two second cousins. It was warm that time of year. I survived on wild berries and I climbed trees for wild nuts. Those who were older would sneak out of the forest to beg or steal corn or potatoes from nearby crops, but I never left. The villages surrounding the forest hated Jews. They'd been fed propaganda that the Jews killed Christ, so they didn't understand us.

In the beginning, it wasn't so bad, but when winter came, it was awful. I had only one dress, a uniform I was issued in the camp. Ten or twelve of us would sleep in some kind of bunker together to keep our bodies from freezing. I don't know how I didn't freeze to death.

When we heard shots, we knew that the Nazis had come into the forest. Everyone ran. They killed my aunt and my male cousin who was seventeen years old. I was shot in the ear and I fainted. It just grazed my ear, but the impact of the explosion threw me on the earth and I was unconscious. I swear I saw my soul go to heaven, white angels and things like that. I thought I was dead and that when you're dead you see yourself go to heaven. Of course, I understand now that I was not conscious. When I came to, I was even more upset. "God, why didn't you finish me off, why didn't you kill me, rather than slowly starve me to death? I have nobody. No parents." I just had my second cousin in the forest with me.

The Nazis came back a second time. We heard shots coming from one side and we ran the other way. I fell through some ice into a body of water that wasn't very deep. My instinct to live was so great that I could still think about how to survive. I covered myself up with branches. I could hear the Ukrainians saying to the Nazis, "Somebody must have been running through there. I can see footprints." And the Nazis said, "I don't want to go that way or we'll fall into the ice too. We'll catch him the next time." My heart stopped beating. I stopped breathing. I waited until I couldn't hear their boots on the ice. I came out of the water with everything frozen on me, including the little dress that I wore until the day we were liberated from the forest.

I got typhus in the forest. I was delirious. My temperature was so high that the strangers I was with in the forest would melt ice on me to try to lower it. They wanted to save my life. I lost all my hair, and I would wear a little handkerchief on my head for warmth. Once, at a conference in New York, a man came up to me and said, "You were in the forest. You didn't have any hair and you wore a red schmatte on your head." I don't know how he recognized me. I was so sick and had stayed in a fetal position so long that I couldn't walk. I thought, "Now I'm really going to die, because when they come into the forest again, I can't run." I don't know what was worse—the fear, the hunger, the lice, or the humiliation.

Springtime came, and then summer, and it was warmer—although to this day, I am still cold. I have not overcome it.

The shooting started and it was coming from both sides. I still couldn't run because I hadn't completely recovered from the typhus. "I do not want to see the face of the Nazis that will shoot me," I thought. I slowly moved from my back to my stomach. "Let them just shoot me in my back or my head and then it'll be over." The shooting stopped and I heard tanks coming into the forest, and I didn't know if they were German or Russian. They were Russian tanks and they had come to liberate us, exactly one year from the day I entered the forest, July 27, 1944.

I went back to my city, and to the homes of the few gentile families to whom my parents gave some of our things. What I wanted most was the photo album. The woman who my family had given it to told me, "You're supposed to be dead. We burned your album." That devastated me, but life goes on. I went to another home and the lady handed me some wool fabric from my parents' department store and a few other things.

I had written to an aunt and uncle I knew were in the United States—in Wilmington, Delaware. Their son found me in a Displaced Persons camp and arranged for me to live with them in Wilmington. They had to guarantee that I would not be a burden on the country. I took an old boat full of children that nearly capsized en route to the U.S. My luggage consisted of two dresses— one I washed and ironed and the other I wore— and the wool fabric, the only thing that my mother once touched.

By then I was seventeen and within three or four days of arriving in Wilmington, I was enrolled in Wilmington High School. I graduated in a year and a half. An uncle from Philadelphia came to my graduation and gave me a $25 graduation gift. That was in 1949, so it was a lot of money in those days.

I knew I wanted to have a suit made from the fabric that had been from my family's store. I went to a tailor on Fourth Street in Wilmington and he charged me $25 for a two-piece suit. I paid him with the graduation money my uncle had given me. I didn't love how it fit, so I only wore the suit a few times, but it hangs in my cedar closet. I always figured I'd be buried in it. But if people can learn from this suit and its history, what difference does it make what I'm buried in?

—AS TOLD TO EMILY SPIVACK

Dorothy Finger is a Holocaust survivor living in Wilmington, Delaware, who lectures extensively about preventing hatred.

James Johnson III

In the old way, the Koyukon Athabascan people of Alaska had a very different approach to the practice of marriage. The chief and elders would choose who would marry within the clan, and this arranged marriage practice was an important part of life for the clan. There was keen interest in keeping bloodlines separate and genetics healthy for the small nomadic population. Even by the age of five, a decision might be made about whom a child would marry when he turned fourteen or fifteen years old.

When Christian priests ventured into the Athabascan territories, a new process that didn't involve arranged marriage was introduced to the Koyukon people. The Christian religion soon became dominant in the region and that religion's traditions became the norm in today's Athabascan marriage ceremonies. My great-grandparents, Hunsleenth and Sneedo (their English names were Martha and George), were among the last couples to be married in the old way. After marriage customs changed to the Christian manner, around the early 1900s, the two renewed their vows.

My 2013 wedding was performed in the Christian way, but elements of the ceremony, including my garb, referenced the customs from when my great-grandparents were married.

A month or so prior to the wedding, my mother and I visited a friend who specialized in making traditional beaded vests, a type of clothing made exclusively for special occasions in Native culture, such as weddings and memorial potlatches. To wear the vest is a symbol of honor and a representation of our Native history.

I decided to have the vest made from cowhide because moose hide has become increasingly difficult to find and expensive to use. The edges of the vest were to be lined with fur and the central areas beaded with intricate floral designs. Athabascan vests are never the same; each one is handmade and represents the skills of the artist.

On the eve of the wedding, my soon-to-be wife, Princess, and her wedding party were already at the wedding destination, Chena Hot Springs Resort, about an hour from were we lived in Fairbanks, Alaska. I ended up staying behind to watch our two boys, prepare my outfit, and complete a lengthy to-do list my fiancée had given me. I couldn't decide if a black or white shirt would look better with my vest so I cleaned two dress shirts and my slacks. I placed both shirts and the slacks in a garment bag. figuring I'd decide on the shirt color the following day. I hung the garment bag in the laundry room right next to the bag with my wedding vest.

I was up until four o'clock in the morning preparing. As a result, I woke up later than anticipated on my wedding day. I raced around, gathering diapers for my son, dancing shoes for my fiancée, and the other items she had requested. I frantically packed up the car and in a final sweep through the house I realized I had almost forgotten the ring! I grabbed it and got on the road with a sense of accomplishment and relief. I was on the home stretch to married life.

I reached the hot springs in just under an hour and had thirty minutes to prepare. I rushed to my best friend's room to put on my outfit. I felt like a rock star whose fans were chanting his name, beckoning him onstage to a sold-out concert. The feeling was surreal and my eagerness was monumental.

But then—you know that sinking feeling you get when you realize you forgot something? Like if there's a sudden drop on an airplane and you're flooded with an anxious, sick feeling? That's what it felt like when I realized what I'd forgotten. In hustling to make sure I had everything, I had only grabbed one garment bag. The other one with my vest was still hanging in the laundry room at home.

I had no idea what to do. Even though people were already filing into the wedding, I thought perhaps I could race back home and postpone the

ceremony for an hour and a half. Or I could call my uncle, who might not have left, and ask him to stop at my house and pick it up, but he didn't have a key. Nothing seemed plausible. I was panicked. My friend said, "Well, I just saw your dad and he's wearing his vest."

In the days leading up to the wedding, my father and I had discussed his attire. He wanted to wear his own vest, one that his mother had made for him. He was a groomsman, and I explained that all groomsmen, including him, were to wear the same white dress shirt and purple tie. I would be the only one wearing a vest for the ceremony. I explained it to him like this: "What if one of Princess's bridesmaids wanted to wear a wedding dress as well? Wouldn't that look out of the ordinary?" My father had relented and everything seemed to be in order.

By the grace of God, my father, a traditional Athabascan elder, had to follow his own traditions, and wore his vest anyway! My friend chased my father down to ask him if I could borrow it, and, of course, he had no objection to handing over his vest to me after he heard about my predicament. I'm six foot one and my dad is five feet six so his vest was snug, but it fit. Crisis averted.

The wedding was a wonderful success. We sang in our Koyukon Native tongue. We did some drumming on a moose hide drum. We joined in a traditional dance where women dance in a circle and men dance in the middle. I saluted my friend for his quick thinking, I praised my father for his good judgment to go against modern symmetry and uphold Native tradition, I honored my grandmother by wearing the vest—and my fiancée said *I do*.

My beautiful vest remains unworn, stored in the same garment bag I had forgotten. Perhaps another occasion will arise to wear it and I can display pride in my cultural heritage. Hopefully that day I won't forget to take the vest with me.

James Johnson III is a program evaluator and substance abuse counselor from Fairbanks, Alaska.

Dustin Yellin

When I found this sweater at a junk shop in England, I was drawn to it, not just because I was an outcast kid growing up in Colorado who had squirrels as friends but, more importantly, because the brand was Avocado. See, in my youth I was a peddler of avocados. My grandfather was in the produce business in downtown Los Angeles, and in the summers of my younger teenage years, I'd work for him. He sold wholesale fruits and vegetables to markets and restaurants and, since the markets opened in the middle of the night, he'd go to work at midnight. Because I was staying with him, I'd go to work, too. He'd drive us to the Produce Place in his Lincoln at ninety miles per hour, listening to Frank Sinatra, swerving, nearly taking people's lives.

I started out stacking boxes of tomatoes and avocados onto pallets, which would be packed onto trucks to get shipped out. I worked my way up. I learned how to use a forklift and load pallets onto the trucks, and then I was actually selling avocados. I'd get avocados at $20 a box and then be like, "Marty, you can have them for $25 a box. Can you believe it? They're so good!" We'd go back and forth. That's the way the produce market works.

My shift went from midnight until ten o'clock in the morning. I'd get home wrecked, pass out, and all I would dream about were avocados. That's why I like wearing this pink sweater with its big Avocado label. My grandfather had wanted me to take over the business. I had a knack for avocados.

I guess it runs in my family. My ninety-year-old grandfather still goes to work every day. He'll die on the avocado floor. But it actually started with my great-grandmother who left Russia for the United States when she was nine years old and began selling fruits and vegetables from a cart in downtown Los Angeles. She grew this little cart into a substantial produce business. For a while, my mom had a shop called Jackie's Green Grocer that sold fruits and vegetables directly to the public. And my uncle has taken over day-to-day operations from my grandfather at the Produce Place.

To this day, I am an avocadoholic. I love them. I was pretty broke when I moved to New York, and I remember going to the deli to get an avocado, a lemon, and a baguette. That was my way to sustain. Now I'm a bit more sophisticated. I get an avocado, salt, and balsamic vinegar.

—AS TOLD TO EMILY SPIVACK

Dustin Yellin is a Brooklyn-based artist and the founder of Pioneer Works, Center for Art and Innovation.

Cynthia Rowley

I joined the Girl Scouts out of boredom. I grew up in a small town in Illinois, population nine thousand, and there wasn't much to do; no summer camp, not really any after school activities. So I became a Girl Scout overachiever, this overzealous badge getter. You had to do an activity to get the badge, and write a little essay about it, and then your mom would sign off on it. Music, art, sports, wilderness, theater, government—I cranked out so many badges that after a while, I didn't even take the time to sew them onto my sash—I just pinned them. Even the badge I got for sewing isn't sewn on!

When I dug this sash out of a box in my basement, I thought, "Wow, look at all those badges!" After all these years, it still made me feel proud of myself.

That Girl Scout structure probably built a lot of my business acumen. I didn't start out with this far-reaching goal of riding in limos with supermodels. I always just thought about one goal at a time, like I just want to figure out how to move beyond being a bartender, I just want to get a picture of my clothes in *Women's Wear Daily*, and so on.

I used to try to jazz up my uniform by hemming it, hiking it up so it was really short, or wearing it with all sorts of belts. I remember marching in a parade in my uniform. I insisted on wearing these black patent leather party shoes with this little heel that made me feel very princess-y. By block two of the parade, the heel had completely fallen off, so I had to limp through the rest of the parade. My parents saw me limping with this nail sticking out of the heel of my shoe, but I waved and was like, *lookin' good*!

When it came to selling cookies, oh my God, I was maniacal. Normally we got clipboards and our little forms with pictures of the cookies and we were supposed to go door-to-door and present ourselves in our uniforms. I remember thinking, it'll take a lot of time if I go to each person's house and wait for her to answer the door, and even then she might not be home. Where can I go and just capture the sales? So I got a card table and set up a little shop, like a little pop-up shop, outside the Jewel grocery store so nobody got in or out without me asking if they wanted to buy cookies. I got tons of orders—tons! But I wound up getting orders that other girls in my troop were trying to get by going door-to-door, so I became a little persona non grata in the troop.

I was a Girl Scout for an embarrassingly long time—until people started teasing me my freshman year of high school when I'd wear my uniform to school on Wednesdays for troop meetings. I was super into it. I can still do the Girl Scout Promise: "On my honor, I will try to do my duty to God and my country, to help other people at all times, and obey the Girl Scout laws." I am such a total dork.

—AS TOLD TO EMILY SPIVACK

Cynthia Rowley is a fashion designer living in New York.

Marina Abramović

I have one piece of clothing I will keep forever and it's the pair of shoes I wore to walk the Great Wall of China. It's the most important clothing I've ever possessed because first, it took eight years for the Chinese to give me permission to walk this wall, and in the meantime, my relationship with Ulay, who was a really big love, was finished, and we decided to walk anyway to say goodbye.

I had to find shoes that were strong enough to protect my ankles because my path to walk the Wall was mainly mountains and was broken in many places. Sometimes I had to use a rope to climb the path, so I had to be very practical. Ulay's section was mostly in the desert, so he needed completely different shoes. I bought my shoes from an alpinist shop. They were made with two types of leather, gave me special protection for my ankles, and had thick soles and thick red laces that I knew I couldn't break because I would never be able to find new ones.

When I put them on I said, "Oh God, it's not going to be easy." It was very hard to walk in them and the first month was hell. I had a huge problem with my knees. But after that they became a part of my entire body, and when I put them on I didn't even feel them anymore.

During the walk, the shoes' soles completely diminished to zero and they became like a second skin. I was walking on different terrain—there'd be iron in the ground, or copper, or other minerals. I noticed that each time I walked on a different type of ground, I felt lighter, calmer, or had more concentration. It came through the shoes, but I felt it throughout my body.

Since that walk twenty-six years ago, I have used the shoes in three performances—*Seven Easy Pieces*, *The House with the Ocean View*, and, during *The Artist Is Present* because the dress was so long that nobody ever saw them.

The second month of *The Artist Is Present* was the most difficult for me. I had on the red dress, and the color was supposed to give me strength. At that time, I had pain in every single muscle of my body and I really doubted if I could make it through the third month. I couldn't even lift my arms up to take my clothes off. It was almost supernatural to me, and I needed to wear the shoes as a support.

The moment I put them on, I have this rush of the memories of everything I've been through, how hard it is to be an artist, and what it takes. And I have this incredible feeling of intimacy, like I'm with an old friend.

When I really want to feel secure and know that things are going to be okay, there are two things I do. I put on these Chinese shoes or I eat baby food. When I feel really shitty, I especially love this special brand of baby food from Holland where I lived for a long time, an instant, bland whole-wheat cereal. When friends come to visit, they know to bring it to me. I also prefer mashed potatoes or, when I'm feeling better, bananas or apples. Sometimes people are ashamed to talk about these things, but I know so many people who would never throw away their old shitty T-shirts or pullovers that are falling apart because of the comfort they get from those clothes. Everybody is vulnerable.

—AS TOLD TO EMILY SPIVACK

Marina Abramović is a performance artist living in New York.

Edith Raymond Locke

I wore this dress on my wedding day, May 26, 1963, to marry Ralph, who has now been my husband for over half a century. Wearing white would have made me feel like an imposter.

Neither of us was intensely religious—I am Jewish, Ralph is Methodist—yet I knew that my father would be happier if a rabbi performed the wedding ceremony. At the time, I was the fashion editor of *Mademoiselle*, and *Women's Wear Daily* ran an item about the wedding entitled, "Guess Who'll Be Walking Down the Church Aisle." My father worked in the garment industry, where *WWD* was the equivalent of the bible, so everyone at work asked him, "Why is Edith walking down a church aisle?" It was just a headline, he told them.

I called many rabbis and none would marry us because we weren't both Jewish; instead, we were married in Chief Justice Gold's chambers in downtown New York.

Scuttlebutt among the fashion crowd in the early sixties had it that a rather fuddy-duddy fashion label called Junior Sophisticates had hired a young new designer named Anne Klein, who was modernizing its image and designing clothes that were chic and classic. I hotfooted it over to 498 Seventh Avenue to see for myself.

I met Anne for the first time on that visit to Junior Sophisticates, and she and I became best friends—long before she became one of America's most influential designers—and continued to be so until her untimely death in 1974. She was one of the few people who knew where I was from, that I had been born in Vienna and escaped the Nazis after the *Anschluss*, just in the nick of time, showing up in New York in 1939 not speaking a word of English. We were the same age, born the same day. From the time I met Anne, she designed almost my entire wardrobe, so it only seemed natural that I would be married in one of Anne's dresses from her Spring 1963 collection.

The label on my wedding dress reads "A Junior Sophisticates Original." It was perfection: a shift made from silk pongee with beautiful Trapunto embroidery. The fabric was ecru, a soft beige, because I only ever wore neutral colors. When I was growing up in Vienna, we had no money, and even though the city was a fashionable place, I could only window-shop on the Graben, the street with the best boutiques. My aunt was an incredible seamstress, and she made my clothes—beautiful, elaborate blouses and pleated skirts, each fold by her hand— but she never used color so I always felt well-dressed in neutral.

When I arrived at the Judge's chambers on my wedding day, Ralph loved the dress. I wore pumps and carried a bouquet of freshly cut Lily of the Valley, brought to me from the country home of my boss, the editor-in-chief of *Mademoiselle*, Betsy Blackwell. My friend, fashion photographer George Barkentin, was one of our witnesses at the ceremony and came as our close friend, not the wedding photographer, so rather unfortunately, there are no photos of me wearing Anne's dress.

Years later, in a moment of folly, I cut and hemmed the dress to tunic length. I thought I'd get more wear out of it over skirts or trousers since hemlines had changed. Because fashion was forever changing and felt disposable back then, I didn't keep any of Anne's clothes. I had just assumed that Anne and her collections would go on forever. But now, Anne is gone, Junior Sophisticates is gone, and the original dress is gone. This shortened version is the only remaining piece of clothing I have that reflects Anne's taste, talent, and desire for perfection. Even though I've "outgrown" its small and slender size, I've never forgiven myself for cutting into Anne's design.

Edith Raymond Locke was a fashion editor at *Mademoiselle* magazine from 1950 to 1971, and editor-in-chief from 1971 to 1980. She lives in Los Angeles, California.

Kathleen Drohan

I've worn this sweatshirt almost every day since I shivered next to my mother's hospital bed nearly six years ago.

After she'd gotten sick, I had imagined myself in my mother's room with Dr. McDreamy or McSteamy tenderly touching my arm as he explained how her last days would progress. I would look lovely in my grief in a simple sundress, my hair pulled back and skin glowing. My mother would be lying serenely and pain free in the room that we would have decorated with tokens from home—a favorite comforter, family photos, flickering candles. She would hold my hand with one of hers and my sister's with the other, telling us how proud she was of us, how much she loved us, and how she'd always be with us. And that she was at peace.

That's how it was supposed to be. That's not how it was.

My hair was dirty when I got the call to come to the hospital. I was wearing a sundress, but an ill-fitting one that had remained clean as my laundry pile grew. Her room was harsh with florescent lights and smelled of the sweet, acrid hospital disinfectant. My mother's serenity was hard to detect behind the tangle of tubes and wires. She looked at me and scratched at her oxygen mask to remove it. In a hoarse voice she whispered, "You're here, too? I know what that means." I waited for more, for her to tell me that I was a welcome sight, not a mere harbinger of her death. All she was able to manage, though, was a call for morphine before it did its job and she was lost in her final slumber.

As the night wore on, I shivered uncontrollably under the air conditioner. A parade of doctors passed in and out of the room. The one I'd named McIHateYou looked at me for a long time before he turned to the machine monitoring her vitals and switched it off. There was no need for it anymore. He left and came back a few moments later, handing me his Harvard Medical School sweatshirt.

I put the sweatshirt on, grateful for its warmth, but I still hated him. I would hate him until he turned the machine back on, turned my mother back on. As the morning arrived, my mother left us. We numbly signed paperwork, gathered her few possessions, and went home.

The next few days were a whirlwind of arrangements. The flurry of well-intentioned loved ones left little time for solitary reflection. When the house quieted at night, I would inevitably find myself reaching for the sweatshirt, cuddling inside the soft, slightly itchy fabric. I didn't wash it until it could practically stand on its own. Though I told myself I would return it to McIHateYou one day, eventually I stopped thinking of it as his, and it became a part of my nighttime routine.

Since that day, I've put on the sweatshirt whenever I'm home alone. I curl up on the couch with tea or, more often, wine. After romantic evenings, when I should be slipping into something lacy, I reach for my sweatshirt. On mornings when I throw it on to run out for coffee and a bagel, I sometimes catch a glimpse of myself in a mirror. I look less like a coed in her boyfriend's sweater, as I imagine myself, and more like a homeless woman in cast-offs. The stains are deeply set in, and its cuffs are frayed, but I can't imagine replacing this sweatshirt.

My mother would have hated it. Most people hate it. I love it.

Kathleen Drohan is a Brooklyn-based freelance writer, publicist, and traveler.

Tiler Peck

I have worn these leg warmers before every single one of my performances with the New York City Ballet—it's become a ritual for me. They're the last things I take off before I go onstage. The most recent performance I was in was George Balanchine's ballet *Symphony in C* and I wore them all the way up until I went on in the fourth movement.

When I perform, it takes me about two hours to get ready. When I do my hair and makeup, I always wear a T-shirt with a cut-off neck (so that I can take it off easily and not mess up my makeup) and a zip-up hoody over my T-shirt. I wear a pair of sweatpants with my legwarmers over them, and booties on my feet, like the kind that skiers wear. The point is to stay really warm to keep my muscles loose. Even after I put my costume on, I keep my legwarmers on until the last possible second so that my muscles are ready to be worked. Sometimes when I'm onstage, I think: "Did I take my legwarmers off?" I'll peek down, relieved that I'm not still wearing them.

I've become known for the legwarmers. Usually, I leave them on top of my bag on the side of the stage when I'm performing, but if they happen to get misplaced or I forget them, someone usually recognizes them as mine. When you're a student at the School of American Ballet, you're not allowed to wear any warm-up clothes. Once you get in to a company, because you're in your dance clothes every day, what you wear to dance in represents your personality. These legwarmers have become my signature. Because I like a bit of routine, I don't feel the same if I don't wear them before every show. I got them in Paris on one of my first company tours with the Ballet, and they've traveled the world with me on every tour since then. No matter where I perform or what ballet I'm in that night, my legwarmers are always the same.

—AS TOLD TO EMILY SPIVACK

Tiler Peck is a principal dancer with the New York City Ballet.

Miss Lisa

I was doing a cute little dance number to Whitney Houston's "It's Not Right, But It's Okay" because the audience always likes to see me do Whitney. Usually I wear something like a bra and panties or a negligee when I dance to her, but that night I decided to wear something different. I performed the number in a chain mail bra and skirt, something I'd worn many times before. Right in the middle of my song I did a twirl, and when I turned back to face the audience, my top had fallen down. I have no idea how it happened.

The audience yelled "Woohoo!" and probably thought I'd done it on purpose, even though I hadn't. Bob and Barbara's has a diverse crowd, so the boys were happy and the girls were like, "Oh my God, you have such perky breasts!" When I started doing drag, I had tiny breasts as I was only on hormones, but eight or nine years ago I got my breasts and hips done in New York so, yes, they are pretty perky.

While you want things to go smoothly, accidents do happen. You deal with it. You tell the audience, "Y'all already know I have breasts, so now y'all just got to see my nipples—get over it!" You can't let it bother you. People are there to see a show, and if I let it get to me, the show is not going to be good.

I finished the number with my hands against my breasts. The audience was impressed. I don't have anything to hide, but regardless, it was shocking and a little embarrassing, especially because just before the show I had reminded the girls who also perform that we don't expose our breasts. I'm strict about it, and I reinforce that before each show.

It's one thing to give the illusion of exposing yourself, which is what I do when I perform. It's another thing to accidentally expose yourself. I've been doing this long enough to know what to wear to prevent mishaps, which is why my top falling off was such a surprise. Before each show, I make sure everything is fastened and secured, so that if I'm wearing a low-cut dress and I'm sweating, my breasts won't pop out. I only wear a spandex dress when I'm doing a slow number. Otherwise, it's going to crawl up and the next thing I know, it's up to my neck and all the audience can see are my panty hose. I don't do cartwheels or splits. If I do splits, everything might come loose that's not supposed to, if you know what I mean.

People ask me where I get my underwear and I tell them I buy it at Home Depot. They look confused, and I tell them that they're my special panties, made of duct tape! But when it's really hot, the adhesive doesn't always stay in place. A friend who sometimes makes my costumes will also make my undies too, to make sure that everything is contained.

After my top fell down last year, I knew I had to retire the chain mail outfit. When I do my numbers, I want to be classy. I want everything to look right on me—my gown, my shoes (spike heels, not platforms or clogs, like some of the other girls), my makeup. It's important that I'm comfortable and that everyone watching the show is comfortable. I make everyone feel welcome. I'll bring anyone up onstage and give him or her attention. I don't judge based on beauty. Everyone is beautiful. That's how I deal with it.

—AS TOLD TO EMILY SPIVACK

Miss Lisa has been the host of Philadelphia's longest-running
drag show for the past twenty years.

Jenna Wortham

Something about the hot pink and teal blue striping of this top made it seem less bingo night and more Christina Applegate in *Don't Tell Mom the Babysitter's Dead*. It was hot. It was very San Francisco circa 2005, the kind of thing that provoked air snaps and emphatic cheers from strangers and random admirers but would have gotten eye rolls in Brooklyn or Manhattan. It got endless compliments anytime I wore it out—in the club, at dinner, on the street—because it invoked the feeling of an occasion, something that brought the party just by wearing it. I liked to tease my curly hair into a tumbleweed-looking shape, add some red lipstick, and put on this shirt.

There's a picture of me wearing the shirt, clutching my best friend, Dwayne. We're both wearing tiny hats that we stole from some cats at a house party. Their owners thought it would be cute to put the cats in tiny cowboy hats. We saw it, *died*, and then decided we needed them for ourselves. I don't know who took the picture or how I got it, but it exists, and it's phenomenal.

I was wearing it when I accidentally drank some pink punch with acid in it during a street parade and then spent the rest of the day lying in the grass in Golden Gate Park. A person in a giant yellow and white duck costume kept running over to gyrate on top of my limp body, and I laughed so hard I almost peed. I probably peed.

I wore it to the dinner party of a friend who worked as a set designer. As expected, her house was impeccably decorated. She invited us all over for a meal, and when we arrived, nothing was prepared. She was wearing only black lingerie and was very, very drunk. She ended up burning the main course. There was so much smoke that the fire department was called and in the confusion, someone dumped a huge glass of wine on the head of an Australian guy who no one seemed to know but who was very nice. It was a ridiculous night and I remember thinking that my fancy sequin shirt was the only thing that I could have possibly worn to something so absurd.

Jenna Wortham is a technology reporter for the *New York Times*.

Andrew Tarlow

I opened Diner in 1998 on the south side of Williamsburg. On the weekends it seemed like the proper thing to do was to wear a suit, to take on the role of restaurateur or maître d'. I had been buying my suits at this great thrift store, Domsey's, which was just around the corner. Considering that the restaurant was in a neighborhood that was fairly rundown at the time, and the dining room was usually filled with people smoking and looking pretty rough, there was this sense of "What are these guys thinking?"

One night during the first year that Diner was open, a woman who'd been helpful in opening the restaurant wore this men's suit to work. It was a busy night. Everyone was running around, but I immediately noticed the suit, and I complimented her on it. It was navy blue and from Brooks Brothers, probably made in the 1960s, with a real collegiate feel to it. She disappeared into the bathroom, and emerged in a completely new outfit. (She was a thrift store aficionado and usually had multiple changes of clothes on her at any time.) She handed me the suit. She just gave it to me. And it fit perfectly.

I wore that suit constantly the first year we were open. And for a while, it felt like I was dressing up something that was a little run down; me, the restaurant, the neighborhood. People weren't expecting much from the food that came out of the kitchen, or that restaurant in general, so we surprised them from the moment I greeted them at the door in my suit.

I don't wear the suit as much these days. And now we have a reputation. We kept raising the bar, and people learned to expect something from us. But back then we had to prove it.

—AS TOLD TO EMILY SPIVACK

Andrew Tarlow is the owner of Diner,
Marlow & Sons, Roman's, the Wythe Hotel,
and Achilles Heel in Brooklyn.

Jeremy Bailey

I started wearing black turtlenecks because I was parodying Steve Jobs's signature look. If you read Walter Isaacson's book about Jobs, it turns out that he owned hundreds of these turtlenecks. He'd taken a trip to Japan and saw how companies like Sony had standard outfits for their employees. He asked fashion designer Issey Miyake, who'd made the Sony outfits, to create an Apple company uniform. While that concept didn't fly with his employees, he had Miyake make him his own black turtleneck uniform. It's fascinating because you assume when you see his turtleneck and dad jeans that he didn't care, but he did, passionately, and he was fully committed to it.

I performed in my black turtleneck from 2004 to 2007, and first tried out a white one in 2008. I was doing a residency in London and hadn't brought a turtleneck, so I had to track one down for an upcoming performance. I bought one at this men's shop that sold gold chains and athletic stuff for beefy guys, but it didn't fit quite right. It's like they just guessed what a human figure looks like when they made it. It hugs the neck and everything flows from there, so I didn't wear it much.

I had just finished reading Steve Martin's *Born Standing Up*, and he explains that the reason he wore his signature white suit was to stand out when he did stadium shows. That way, people could see his gestures better since his jokes were often tied to his body. I thought I'd wear white and aspire to have a stadium show one day, too, just like Steve Martin, even though I typically perform to a room with a smattering of people. I found the perfect turtleneck at a thrift store in Vancouver, British Columbia, but once I had it, I just held on to it. I wasn't ready to wear it yet.

I'm half Ukrainian and went to do a residency in Ukraine to make a work that involved augmented reality and wearable sculpture. I needed to wear a uniform color because the piece was more about the sculpture and less about me—I would become a canvas or gallery wall. I had packed both a black and white turtleneck, but once I was in this dirty factory space where I had my studio, white made more sense. In science fiction, the future is always white, clean, and contained. I had read another book, called *Chromophobia*, by David Batchelor, around this time, and he described how the modernist design aesthetic— the white kitchen, white floors, white walls—is a denial of our humanity. The reason bathrooms are white, too, is not only so you know that they are clean, but also so you know that they are not what's inside of us. I couldn't think of a place that was more like a symbol of containment of vile human insides than this rural depressed village in Ukraine. There was no way for me to not feel imperialistically privileged even though genetically it is where I'm from. For my performance, I wore the white turtleneck with white long underwear because I hadn't decided what the future of the waist down might be. The long underwear would at least signify that I hadn't really figured it out yet.

Shortly thereafter, I determined that I should wear jorts with my white turtleneck. Steve Jobs wore those ill-fitting jeans, so, in keeping with my initial inspiration, I wore jorts that are a little bit too tight. I like the contrast: feminizing my exposed legs in the context of my own sexual ambiguity, paired with the androgyny of a full-coverage turtleneck.

In the past three or four years since I've been wearing this outfit, I've become much more confident about the persona I am presenting. When I put on this outfit to perform, I transform from Jeremy Bailey, regular guy, to Jeremy Bailey, Famous New Media Artist.

Wearing a white turtleneck does pose a few challenges. It's not necessarily the most comfortable thing because you always feel like you have a little angel strangling you, although that tension on your neck could be comforting if you have an asphyxiation fetish. And I have to bleach it constantly. My wife can confirm that I never sweat, but dirt has accumulated, especially since I've been performing exclusively in this white turtleneck for three years.

The story of this not-so-original outfit took over ten years to conceive, and I probably could have hired a stylist who'd say, "Of course—let's pull some jorts and a turtleneck and it will be a satire of a mom and a new media artist all at once." But I agonize over these decisions because I know it is part of a body of work, of creating a fictional career for people to enjoy, of making everyday decisions that accumulate into a lifelong performance.

—AS TOLD TO EMILY SPIVACK

Jeremy Bailey is a new media artist living in Toronto.

Brian Droitcour

When I came to my senses I was handcuffed, sitting on a curb in the parking garage of the Miami Beach police department, and wearing a green tank top that said *Nice Smile*, which had been given to me a few weeks earlier by my friend Timmy. I couldn't remember putting the tank top on but I remembered that I had planned to. It was December 2007 and I was in Miami Beach for Art Basel, so I'd been wearing smart-looking, light-colored button-downs every day to look professional at the fair and at the receptions and cocktail hours in the evenings. On the last night I wanted to go with my friends to Twist, a club three blocks from my hotel. My plan was to stop in my room and change into the *Nice Smile* tank. Apparently I had done just that, but the last thing I remembered was eleven o'clock at night at the *Artforum* party, drinking cocktails and having a great time in my white collared shirt.

"Trying to give me AIDS," I heard a man say. It was a police officer, blond with a squareish, solid build. He grabbed a paper towel and rubbed his face. I felt like his words were directed at me—as a question or an accusation.

"What?" I said. My brow furrowed in an automated expression of confusion as I tried to process his words and my surroundings. In doing so, I felt a sudden numbness in my face, and then a trickle of liquid around my lips. I tasted blood.

I looked around. Besides the blond guy there were three other police officers. They were looking back at me, but when I came close to making eye contact, they'd turn away. The blond one was rubbing his knuckles. The cops looked at each other, and then at me. There was a pause.

"Do you know why you're here?" asked the blond one.

I didn't. My last memory was the *Artforum* party.

"Well…," said the police officer. He tossed the paper towel and turned to face me. "You killed

a man," he said, pacing in front of me. "A homeless guy sitting outside of Twist kept asking you to suck his dick. And you got sick of it. So you picked up a rock and threw it at his head. Cracked his skull and he died. Because you didn't want to suck his dick."

I swallowed, automatically, and tasted blood again. "I killed someone?" I said softly. I was already in pain, but suddenly I felt exhausted. My head dropped to my chest. That's what had happened? That's why I was here? I had nothing to say. I'd been blackout drunk and had stupid, bad things happen to me because of it before—lots of times. But now I'd become a murderer. I was responsible for a man's death. Drinking ruined my life, and worse, someone else had lost his because of it. Now I would go to jail for—what, ten or twenty years?

A stocky, dark-haired cop who had been writing the whole time put down his pen. He had finished the report, and they were ready to send me to jail. A different dark-haired officer was my escort. He helped me stand, pushed me into the backseat of a police car, and drove me out of the station. It was about six in the morning and the sun was rising. It shined through the back window and I squinted, the pain of the light in my eyes distracting me from the pain in my face around them. I kept thinking about how I would now be spending the next few decades of my life. The officer said nothing to me.

When we got to the jail we passed through a series of secure doors. My handcuffs were removed and I was checked in. My escort handed the police report to me, and I read it. It said that I had passed out on the sidewalk, and when paramedics came to revive me I had struggled. The police subdued me, and I struggled some more, so they arrested and tased me. I scanned it again, on both sides, for a mention of the homeless man and the murder, but found nothing. Instead I had been charged with two counts of assaulting a police officer. I looked

up at the dark-haired cop who was filling out some paperwork. "It doesn't…It doesn't say anything about killing anyone here," I said.

The officer didn't look at me but he shook his head and sighed. "He was just fucking with you."

Relief that it hadn't happened and shock at the story's invention hit me at once, and it kept me in a semicatatonic state of confusion for several minutes, through my processing and my mug shot. I imagined myself picking up a rock from the street and throwing it at a man's head—but there weren't really rocks littering the streets of South Beach big enough to kill someone, were there? And so, in the midst of these thoughts, I have a look of slack-jawed distraction in my mug shot, which shows up easily when you search for me on Google Images.

In the same image, although my eyes are cast down, my left eyebrow jerks upward and my nose bends to the side. The blond cop had asked me if I had AIDS, and when I didn't respond, he kept asking, until I spit in his face. He then punched me a few times, which is when I slumped down to the curb and came to. I also look shirtless in the mug shot because the *Nice Smile* tank has a very wide neckline, and you can just barely see the top's shoulder straps in the corners. It wasn't much to be wearing in the heavily air-conditioned Miami jail. I was chilly there for the next fourteen hours until I was released on bail, paid by my parents.

Brian Droitcour is an art critic and an editor at the *New Inquiry*.

Lindsey Thornburg

I first saw the psychedelic patterns, insane colors, and layers of fabric worn by the indigenous people of Peru during a trip to Machu Picchu. Although it might sound like a stretch, somehow it seemed really transferable to a city environment like New York.

I grew up in Montana and Colorado, and the only American brand I could think of that had any similarity to the textiles I'd seen in Peru was Pendleton, which made these graphic, Native American–inspired blankets. The next time I was at my dad's house in Montana, I asked him if I could have my grandfather's Pendleton blanket. He agreed.

At the time, I had a Scottish walking cloak, and I couldn't really afford anything nicer. I took that cloak, refined the design, and used my grandfather's blanket to make this cloak. I started making a few each week, all based on this original cloak, and selling them out of friends' stores. In November 2008 the *New York Times* covered them in the Sunday Styles section and they just took off. That was during the recession, but my inbox was full of women, aged from nineteen to sixty-five years old, who wanted the cloaks to stay warm, to essentially walk around wrapped in a blanket.

Everyone who placed an order wanted this one silhouette, the one that I had created from my grandfather's Pendleton blanket. I had a Korean sewer who I'd been working with make my samples. He saw my company growing, but he made me use the one paper pattern we used for the first cloak. He would take it, kiss it, kiss my forehead, and say, "This piece of paper changed your life. This is good luck. Don't ever *not* use this piece of paper." For three years we used that one piece of paper to design every single cloak.

I caught some flack at one point because Native Americans believe that you must maintain the integrity of Pendleton blankets, and that if you cut into them, you let the spirits out. I had to prove to them that I was maintaining the integrity while cutting into the blankets, that I was letting the spirits live by keeping people warm rather than remaining folded on your parents' guest bed.

I've made minor tweaks to the design each year, but essentially it's the same garment since I began in 2007. Sometimes I wonder if it's weird to be so passionate about one thing and to develop a company around it, but I like making one thing and making it awesome.

—AS TOLD TO EMILY SPIVACK

Lindsey Thornburg is a fashion designer living in New York.

Kitty Stryker

Every time the plane approached Heathrow Airport and I saw the London skyline, it brought tears to my eyes. Then I'd scold myself for being so sentimental. Usually the first thing I'd see was the London Eye, then Big Ben, and then maybe the Gherkin. I lived in London for four years and spent a lot of time near Liverpool Street under the shadow of that great phallic symbol. After one drunken night I made a friend lick it—it was the grossest thing ever.

It was March 2012 and my visa had expired so I was moving away. It was getting close to the Olympics, and I hate crowds and sports. I was happy to return to San Francisco and get away from all of that chaos. Before I left, I went shopping at Marks & Spencer for tights, thigh highs, and lingerie because, as a size twenty, it's hard for me to find cute clothes in the U.S. I saw these stockings with the London skyline in silhouette, and I was so excited by the image that I bought three pairs. Whenever I wore them, people would ask if my legs were tattooed. I felt giddy, connected to London and to my fiancé, whom I desperately missed.

I had expected to visit again in October to see my fiancé. We were to be married the next spring and had planned to stay there permanently. Instead we broke up over Google Chat. It was both incredibly personal and completely dispassionate at the same time—I guess technology can do that. I mailed the ring back to him and wept for days.

The breakup was like fanning away the London fog from around our relationship, and I saw it starkly for what it was: abusive and unhealthy. I couldn't admit that when we were together; I loved the fairy tale too much. Mourning him was wrapped in my mourning the chance to return to London. It was difficult to tell which loss hurt more.

That sense of longing hasn't gone away. It's been two years since I last lived in the city I loved. Two pairs of the stockings have gotten runs and are almost unwearable. Like my time in London, this last pair is precious.

Kitty Stryker is a marketing manager and queer porn performer.

Andrew Kuo

The Simpsons came out when I was a really young teenager, and Canal Street was the spot to find all the new, bootleg Bart stuff. My mom would give me $20, I'd eat lunch in Chinatown, and then I'd buy fireworks and a bunch of Bart T-shirts on Canal: Bart Blackman, Bart Marley, Bart as Max Headroom, Buckwheat Bart. Loads of mash-ups and various degrees of reappropriation—Bart as Max Headroom saying "Cowabunga dude!" like the Teenage Mutant Ninja Turtles. I think that was the golden age of mash-ups, when people could pirate Photoshop or Illustrator and make their own T-shirts, fliers, or logos. You didn't know what was real and what wasn't, and it didn't really matter. I loved basketball so I was really into the Air Bartman shirts with the Jumpman logo. I've since lost them all or my mom got rid of them, except for one Air Bartman shirt.

I'm a lifelong Knicks fan and when Linsanity happened in 2012, it was a really emotional thing for me. Not only was it a rags-to-riches, David and Goliath kind of story, but it was also an Asian dude doing it! He wasn't especially tall or fast, but he took the city, my favorite city, by storm. It was spring and getting warmer, and I'd walk down the street and people would be like, "Jeremy Lin—is he playing tonight?" Construction workers, people behind the counter at bodegas, everyone was like "Jeremy Lin, Jeremy Lin!" Growing up in New York, I saw divisive moments, but Linsanity brought the city together.

At the same time, an undercurrent of weirdness got tapped into with Linsanity. You'd see references to chopsticks and slanted eyes and, while it wasn't really racist, I didn't appreciate the sentiment. I wanted to make something about this moment in time and I recalled those Bart Blackman shirts from the eighties that had sparked a controversy when they came out.

Using the Air Bartman shirt I'd held on to as a model, I made this Lin T-shirt—in fact, I printed quite a few of them—and gave them away to anyone who wanted one, which is what I do with all the shirts I make.

I thought it was perfect. A yellow character that was a nonracist version of the moment, that also tipped my hat to my childhood and to a character that previously had been used to talk about racially sensitive issues. Linsanity uncovered prejudices I encountered growing up Asian. Jeremy Lin headlines like "Who said Asians can't drive" and "Chink in the armor" reinforced how the public thinks about Asian people, sometimes true, sometimes not. I don't know if the craziness around Linsanity would have happened if he was white.

It only lasted a few weeks. They worked him too hard, and then he hurt his knee. He got traded to Houston, and the madness was over. It was heartbreaking, and I made another T-shirt about that moment so that I could relax myself—Bart Simpson drinking a purple drink and saying, "Don't have a cow, man!"

—AS TOLD TO EMILY SPIVACK

Andrew Kuo is an artist and contributor to the *New York Times*.

Davy Rothbart

I picked a guy up just past Flagstaff, a tiny, grizzled man on the shoulder of Highway 64 with his thumb out, wearing a backpack bigger than himself. I stopped, and he waddled toward me, a tin canteen dangling from his pack. Next to that, I noticed, was this pair of hiking boots, hanging by their laces.

The guy's face was creased and smudged and he thrust out his hand: "Young man, thanks for stopping! Name's John. Where ya headed?"

"The Grand Canyon," I said.

"Bingo! Me too!"

Headed west in the car, John told me that he'd worked in a machine shop in Lowell, Massachusetts, for thirty-five years, but his lifelong dream was to visit the Grand Canyon. He'd read dozens of books about it, studied its geology and its history; he'd even surrounded his bed with pictures cut out of *National Geographic*.

John said he always talked about the Grand Canyon, even at work, and a few weeks ago one of the guys in the shop said: "For Chrissakes, shut up already! Grand Canyon this, Grand Canyon that. You'll never make it there."

So John said: "Okay, I quit." He turned in his tools, walked out, and scraped together enough money for a Greyhound ticket to Amarillo. He said goodbye to his mother and his teenage son, who shared his apartment, and hopped on the bus.

It took him three days to reach Amarillo and three more days to hitchhike to Flagstaff. Now that we were closing in on the Canyon itself, he was shaking with excitement. "I can't believe we'll be there in less than two hours," he said. He clapped his hands. He drummed on the dashboard. He whistled at the sight of each towering cactus we passed.

Then he peered at me. "Say, you're pretty quiet. What are you brooding about?" I told him about my broken heart, the girlfriend who'd moved to Scotland, how I hadn't dated or kissed another girl in two years. "I've never been more lost," I said.

John just nodded, like he understood. I took comfort that I was about to witness someone realize his lifelong dream. We passed the ranger station at the outer perimeter of the park, and for the next twelve miles, as we approached the edge, John leaned halfway out his window like a happy hound.

I've never seen an old man move so fast as when we reached the first overlook, and John bounded from the car and sprinted toward the edge to gaze across the vast chasm. He turned back toward me, eyes wet, face shining.

We hiked an hour down into the canyon as the sun lowered. John's book learning about the canyon had worked; he enthusiastically pointed out rocks and wildlife, full of information. John the machine-shop worker from Lowell had become a radiant expert on the Grand Canyon. He fell into a contented silence, and we returned to the rim. The canyon hummed at our backs. We found a campground, pitched a tent in the dark, and shared a canteen full of whiskey as it started to snow.

In the morning, we went to the park office. John was here, but now what? He had no money, or place to stay. We thought he could stir up a job working trail maintenance. The head ranger, astonished at his depth of knowledge, hired him on the spot. I bought John a few days of groceries and paid for his campsite through the weekend, to tide him over.

In return, John offered me his hiking boots. "Take 'em," he said, before I could protest. "They don't fit me. I got the ugliest blisters you ever seen. I'll be better in sneakers." What he meant, I realized, was that he'd reached his destination, and I hadn't. There was farther for me to go, and I needed those boots more than him. He was right. I wore them for years.

Davy Rothbart is the creator of *Found* magazine, a contributor to public radio's *This American Life*, a documentary filmmaker, and the author of *My Heart Is an Idiot*.

Maira Kalman

I got this apple green sweater from my mother, Sara.
I wore this when I went to Tel Aviv with her.

It means something to me because I adored my
mother and she liked how I looked in it. I wore it
so much that the elbow was completely worn away.
I cut a little piece of another sweater (grey with
buttons) and patched the elbow with it.

It is my lucky sweater because I always need
luck. And the feeling of being lucky, which is ridiculous and elusive, is still a pleasant one.

Maira Kalman is an author, illustrator, designer, and artist who
has written and illustrated seventeen children's books.
Her books for adults include *The Principles of Uncertainty*
and the illustrated edition of William Strunk Jr. and
E. B. White's *The Elements of Style*.

Tito

I was formally introduced to Dapper Dan by Eric B. and Rakim in the mideighties. I was a Harlemite in the music business, so I knew about him making custom gear at his store on 125th Street. At the time I didn't have anything, resource-wise, to facilitate getting something made by Dap. Dap was like Gucci in Harlem, like Bloomingdale's. People didn't really care about buying stuff from Gucci when they could get something custom-made from Dap, especially if they could get a version of something he'd made for Mike Tyson or the most glamorized hustler in the neighborhood—just to say that they had a Dapper Dan piece.

About a year after I met Dap, I had the resources to buy something from him. The second piece of probably ten pieces he made for me was a double-breasted Polo trench. I'd go into his store and say, "I want this cut, I want a blazer top, I want it double-breasted, I want a Sherlock Holmes hat with earflaps to match, and I want a pair of sneakers wrapped in the same kind of leather," and he could make that happen. He could make that happen within a week. If you needed it sooner and you had the resources, he'd say, "Let me go in the back, talk to my team, and see what I can do," and he'd make it happen within twenty-four hours. And one of the dopest things was that nobody was going to have the same jacket. He'd tell people that he could make something similar, but that he wouldn't make the exact same thing. It was a one-of-a-kind joint.

He made me this trench for a show at Madison Square Garden. I was nineteen or twenty—just a little boy. What makes it crazy is that I wasn't even performing that night. It wasn't a hip-hop show;

it was a really big R&B show with New Edition, LeVert, Bobby Brown, and Heavy D & the Boyz. MSG was the place where everybody would congregate. I'd be backstage, for sure. These performers knew me and had a lot of love for me. I had been on tour with Doug E. Fresh, and people had also gotten it into their heads that I was Heavy D's little brother, which sounded good to me!

I had what I called my awards show outfits. I'd get pictures taken in them and wouldn't wear them again. This trench was one of those pieces. I had it made just for that night. People would be like, "What are you doing? Are you serious?" Basically, you'd go, get your picture taken, get your marketing up, and let cats know that you're still in the business.

I'd been making statements with my clothes since the Fearless Four era. I always added certain details; embroider some parts, put fur on other parts. I'd wear Bally's with leather bomber jackets and leather pants, when they were in style, and this was all before Dap. I had a presence in the industry; I was under the radar, but still respected. When I started going to Dapper Dan, it took my style to the fifth power. If I had a double-breasted peacoat, I would take it to Dap and say, "I want mink on the collar, mink on the sleeves, mink around the bottom, and mink on the trim." This was during a time when fur was big. I wouldn't do that now, but back then, I was trying to outshine whatever was going on. I always wanted to be a little different, and I had this name I had to live up to. I would walk in wearing the type of shit that performers would be wearing, and people would look at me like, "Yo, who is he?"

—AS TOLD TO EMILY SPIVACK

Tito was a member of the hip-hop group the Fearless Four.

Dapper Dan

It was 1972, right after the Nicky Barnes and Frank Lucas drug epidemic. Everybody in Harlem wanted to be fly. The movie *Super Fly* had just come out, and, because it took place in Harlem, it both captured the essence of the street and inspired everyone in the street. The actors were all dressed in super fly Harlem fashions. There's a scene where Ron O'Neal, the main character, is in a club in Harlem and he's wearing this exact coat! I'd bought mine on Delancey Street because that's where all the Jewish immigrants sold suede and leather, and you could get a good deal, but I'd bought it before the movie came out. People noticed that it was the same coat as the one in the movie, and it just gave me this automatic street rep. I got so much respect.

I was at an interesting stage in my life at that time, at a crossroads. I was a full participant in street activities prior to the midsixties. It's where I got my basic training. Everybody was selling drugs. I sold drugs. But I saw how it was cursed, how it turned brother against brother. Around 1967 I went out of circulation for about three years. I went back to school, got my GED, later graduated from prep school, and then attended Iona College. I was studying and finding out who I was. I spent time in Africa in 1968, and when I got back I was ready for the street again, but this time, my whole life had changed. I had an education and a higher spiritual sensibility. I had read *The Teachings of Don Juan: A Yaqui Way of Knowledge*, by Carlos Castaneda, learned about transcendental meditation, and listened to The Beatles. The Beatles were exploring their spiritual substance and we were finding out about our color, our cultural identity. I went to Black Panther meetings, got involved with the Nation of Islam movement and the Five-Percent Nation. I knew I needed to stay close to my own spiritual substance, but the street kept pulling me. I still wanted to be fly, especially because I'd never been fly.

To understand what a garment like this does to a person, you have to have had holes in your shoes. As kids growing up in Harlem, we all had holes in our shoes. We used to stuff newspaper in them. If you walked down the street you would see little scraps of newspaper wherever a bunch of kids in my neighborhood went. Then we got creative and started cutting linoleum and putting it inside our shoes. No matter what—holes in our shoes, holes in our socks—we tried to look the best we could because positive self-esteem made a difference.

In the early seventies, I was back on the street, but I knew I wouldn't get lost. I was driving around in a Mercedes Benz, wearing silk pastel-colored suits—soft yellow, sky blue, mint green—and this coat. I was a professional gambler at the time. I'd say, "They want to win me. I want to win money." I was cultivating a persona. When the guy I had been named after came out of prison, he said, "I'm not Dapper Dan no more. I'm Tenor Man Dan and *you* are Dapper Dan." It was because of what I had learned on the street. I was knowingly playing into the values around me. Guys would see me all put together and that's ultimately why, years later, they wanted to come into my store. Meanwhile, I didn't want to end up like the original Dapper Dan, and I found myself slowly retreating from the scene, from the street. I went back to Africa. My moral judgment was developing. It got to a point where I couldn't gamble anymore.

I wore this coat to Madison Square Garden in 1972 to see Sly and the Family Stone. A few of us went and we took our wives. We could barely get tickets because Sly was off the meter at that time. And the whole audience was white! When Sly went, "Let me take you higher!" the audience was jumping up and screaming "Hiiiigher!" I'd never seen a black guy take white guys there. Maybe Jimi Hendrix at Woodstock? But Sly was *it*.

I was still wearing this coat when I opened Dapper Dan's Boutique in 1982, although I wouldn't wear it to the store. While I was working, I only wore clothes I sold at the store, clothes with street credibility that were influenced by hustlers and sought after by musicians and people with money and power. I knew they were looking to me, and I wore what I knew they wanted. I've always been good at dressing according to the occasion: I'd adapt my style to my shop, a club, or going downtown. But this coat, now more than forty years old, will always represent me and this whole journey.

—AS TOLD TO EMILY SPIVACK

Dapper Dan is a fashion innovator from Harlem who created custom luxury pieces for hip-hop artists, athletes, and gangsters in the 1980s.

Sasha Frere-Jones

For a long time, I simply didn't know how to dress. As a teen, I didn't feel tough enough to be a punk. I didn't want to slam dance or get hit on the head or spit at people, so there was no reason to wear a uniform that implied I wanted to do any of that stuff. I also didn't want to identify as a skinhead—even after I had shaved my head—because I'd heard about some alliance between Oi! and the National Front or some larger, unnamed racist group. Since I only got news on this stuff from British music weeklies, which only appeared occasionally, I decided to skip all the punk symbols.

I loved The Jam, who seemed to be flag bearers for mod as far as a teenager in New York could tell. The tweaked classicism of mod made it seem like a style cohort that was relevant to vague ideas I had of myself—and these were deeply vague. But I couldn't afford tapered trousers or a scooter, so the best I could do was to wear a long green canvas trench coat, which I bought after seeing *Quadrophenia*. I am half English by birth but was raised in Brooklyn; without the right accent, the coat made sense for about a week.

Later, in college, when I was in a band, I bought creepers with floral print uppers. I thought these would be part of my onstage look. I thought they were badass and subverted the dominant macho rockabilly style, but yet again, they could do this only for someone else. They should have been on the feet of someone in Prince's band, maybe, but not at the end of my legs. In these shoes, I looked 90 percent person and 10 percent crumpled gift wrap. The shoes gathered dust, and eventually went to a girlfriend who swore she would stuff the toes with tissue paper and wear them.

But when I was thirteen, I bought a vintage band jacket from Canal Jeans, when it was still located on Canal Street. That was the year my parents were taking me to England. I'd been dying to go. MTV didn't exist yet but music videos had just started. I'd seen a clip for David Bowie's "Ashes to

Ashes," and I was all jangled up. Music felt new and brighter, and England seemed to be where all the lights were turned on.

I walked around Camden Market and bought patches of bands I liked, to sew onto my jacket. I got Sergeant Peppers because I thought I was in The Beatles when I wore the jacket; Blondie; The Selecter; The Rolling Stones; and a Union Jack to go across the back. I was effectively asking everybody in the world to beat me up, but nobody did.

When I returned to New York, I wore it to school and felt like a clown. This was because I looked like a green clown in an overly big jacket that some advertising firm had rented, spackled with logos, and thrown out.

Clothes are a language; this jacket was incoherent. It certainly wasn't sending any effective signals to other people wearing green vintage band jackets. It was, at best, an experiment in using clothes to figure out how I appeared in the world, concretely, to others, and what I sounded like, visually. That's how I thought of it, how I sounded through what I wore.

I was naive to think that a piece of clothing could turn me into a person, especially since I hadn't decided who that person was. Part of me thought I would suddenly be in the Buzzcocks if I wore the right T-shirt, even though I hadn't sorted out if I even wanted to be in the Buzzcocks. But the minute I got into the world, I realized, nope, it's just me, wearing something extremely yellow with a funny name on it. Mocking was more or less as bad as nobody getting the point.

There's a great documentary called *Dirty Girls*, about high school girls in the nineties who dyed their hair funny and were the "different" girls in their social universe. They were submitted to some fairly brutal ostracism. Like those girls in the documentary, some kids have a hard time in high school, or at some point in their lives, and they need clothes to act as a force field around them, either

to set themselves apart or to join the goofballs, the Jay Z fans, the Star Wars nerds. I was never that unhappy, never an actual weird kid who needed armor. Whenever I tried joining a cohort with my clothing, it was trouble that led nowhere, neither placing me in a new peer group nor throwing me out of the village. I was missing that psychotic teenage flair and the upkeep was too much, so eventually I'd run out of steam and wear a combination of minimalist Christmas gifts, hand-me-downs from Dad (the most stylish category), and the few clothes my summer salary afforded me.

I came close to finding my cohort when hip-hop was just beginning to kick in. I started wearing jeans, mesh hats, and black referee sneakers with fat red laces. That lasted for a little while. But it was only in the last five years, as an adult, that I realized that I could wear tailored clothing with good boots and look like I resembled my own thoughts. I'd basically been waiting to be a grown-up, for a moment when my clothes weren't just a mute default position.

A few years ago, I gave my thirteen-year-old son the green jacket. Two badges were added for his two favorite football teams, Chelsea and Liverpool. He wore it out once, and returned in fifteen minutes. "Dad," he said, "I can't be outside wearing this thing."

—AS TOLD TO EMILY SPIVACK

Sasha Frere-Jones is a staff writer for the *New Yorker* and cofounder of the BATAN Arts Collective.

Tamara Santibanez

I never had a leather jacket growing up. An item of clothing so definitive, so essential for a young punk, and yet I went without one for years. Sure, I was suited up in a pair of Doc Marten combat boots that lasted me from age fifteen to twenty-two. But when you measure in at a whopping five feet two, a well-fitting leather is hard to come by. As a result, I cultivated a profound interest in the Punk Vest, poring over images of painted, studded, and destroyed vests across all subcultural genres, from biker colors to Hesher denims with heavily embroidered Maiden patch coverage to the infamous Manson vest.

To this day I have a large collection of my own handmade vests. The collection includes a leather version—with *Fuck the World* painted on the back in Wite-out and a smoking skull with circle *A* eyes—that tends to get me into trouble (see: the time I wore it to the airport); a classic sleeveless acid-wash style with skate punk patches sewn on the back; a denim one with a God's eye–like appliqué that elicits compliments from hippies and fashion folks alike; and a veritable timeline of accompanying pins, patches, studs, and fabrics that chronicle my transition from street punk to crust punk to black metal aficionado to leather mama, and so on. As a vegetarian and vegan for a decade,

I didn't seek out the mythical leather jacket because I was morally opposed, and by the time I considered bringing the material back into my life, I had given up on ever finding one that was my size.

Last year I attended a dinner party, and at the end of the evening my best friend informed me that she had a belated birthday gift for me. She disappeared from the room, and then reappeared with the smallest adult leather jacket I had ever seen. Perfect classic motorcycle styling, snaps, zippers, collar; it was everything I had ever wanted. The jacket fit like a dream. As the story goes, one of our friends had found it while thrifting. She bought it, realized it was too small for her, and then passed it around the more petite members of our social circle, until my friend Emily snagged it and gave it to me. I have treasured it ever since.

It's cliché, really, but throwing it on makes me instantly *cooler*. I have shown remarkable restraint with adorning it—I suffer from what an ex once termed "flair addiction"—and the spiked studded shoulders invite more touching from strangers than I prefer. But it doesn't matter. I have finally become one of those punks I used to mock out of jealousy, who, despite eighty-degree heat, wears her really tough, nonbreathable leather jacket-turned-security blanket.

Tamara Santibanez is a visual and tattoo artist living in Brooklyn.

Courtney Maum

My father's Ralph Lauren cardigan is age-stained and moth-nibbled, and the cuffs are all stretched out. Although I have no recollection of my father wearing it, it corresponds to the type of man he was when he was still married to my mother: a long-legged, rare-steak eating, tennis-playing man who belonged to clubs with letterpressed stationery in royal blue and cream. He wore Fila windbreakers and white swimsuits and he listened to the Bee-Gees. He liked his swimming pools hot.

My father is not this man any longer. The change started when I entered high school, when I was living with him and his new wife. They were trying to have babies. They were trying to rebrand. They sold the oriental carpets and the uncomfortable antique furniture my mother favored, and they upholstered a sectional sofa entirely in fleece. They started using the word "rec room" really often. My dad got an eBay account and spent his free time bidding on reinforced athletic socks and synthetic fur throws.

When I was in tenth grade, they upgraded from a CD player that could hold three discs to one that could hold six. They loaded it with new wave country music: Tim McGraw, Lady Antebellum, Rascal Flatts. By the time I graduated high school, they'd had three new children. My father added a turquoise bear paw to my stepmother's silver feather charm bracelet for every kid. I went off to college. I majored in comparative literature. And then I moved to France.

By the time I moved back to the U.S. in 2005, my dad and stepmom had relocated from Greenwich, Connecticut, to Chattanooga, Tennessee. The memories of my father as a man who belonged more—stylistically speaking—to "heroin collegiate" than "country casual" became incongruous with the person who had my old piano bench reupholstered with his favorite pair of jeans.

The first time my parents met my now-husband, the airline had lost his luggage on our flight over from France. He showed up at my father's house in a thin shirt and a light jacket, shivering from meet-the-American-parents-nerves and a cold caught on the plane. My father came down the staircase shouting, "Diego's gonna love this," old cardigan in hand.

Diego put the sweater on in front of my step-mother and father. They both said it looked great. The arms dangled a little bit and one of the white buttons fell to the floor when Diego tried to button it, but it did look great.

I was really jealous when my dad gave him that sweater. It suited Diego's style perfectly and, aside from being a little large on him, it was an appropriate gift. All my life, my father never seemed to "get" me, and his lack of comprehension was manifested by absurdly impractical presents. For my sixteenth birthday he tried to give me a Vietnamese potbellied pig that belonged to a neighbor. Another year, at Christmas, he gave me a printout of an item he'd won for me on eBay: a giant, wooden canoe. It was located in Ithaca, New York. "Pick up only." I lived in Brooklyn at the time, five hours away from it, and nowhere near a lake.

I instilled a lot of meaning into the handing over of that sweater. I felt like my father recognized something in Diego that he'd never been able to connect with in me. But now I've come to learn the reasons behind some of his odder presents. The pig, for example, was part of a revenge plan against my mother for getting so much alimony because she had custody of me at the time, and thus, she would be the pig's primary caretaker. It had never occurred to him that I'd turn it down. I realize now that the sweater was just a three-pound, thick-knit relic he wanted out of the house.

In the last couple of years, my father has started referring to me in conversation as "our oldest" or "our daughter" when introducing me to people I've never met. He'll say this with his arm around my stepmother, and I don't interject. I'm sure it would be more convenient for them if I was their daughter. In his perfect world, I'd be the kind of girl who loves Taylor Swift and has red hair and grey eyes like his other kids. Instead, I'm a dark-haired, Taylor Swift–despising reminder of a past he can't rewrite.

I spent a lot of time—a decade—being angry with my father because he cheated on my mother with a woman he loved more. And then I fell out of love with someone who still loved me, and I experienced what it was like to live inside the emptiest version of myself. Today, I try to find the humor in my father's missteps. I want to forgive him.

Sometimes I take the sweater out of my husband's closet and put it on. I move around the house in it, like a child playing dress up. Like a child playing house.

Courtney Maum is the author of the novel *I Am Having So Much Fun Here Without You*, a humor columnist, and corporate namer. She splits her time between the Berkshires, New York, and Paris.

John Hodgman

I have a dress and I have worn it many times.

I needed to impersonate a dead author for Paul F. Tompkins's *Dead Authors* podcast. Most of the good authors on the list he gave me had already been taken, meaning someone else had done Jorge Luis Borges. I was scanning through the list of these garbage authors and my eyes lit upon one that came as a complete revelation to me; of course, I should be Ayn Rand. In the podcast, Tompkins, in the guise of legendary time-traveling writer H. G. Wells, interviews various dead authors by bringing them forward in his time machine to discuss their lives and work. I'd been fascinated with Rand since I'd written a story in the *New York Times* magazine about a competitive championship tournament bridge player who was also an active objectivist and Rand devotee. I had read half of *Atlas Shrugged* before I got the gist of my role. I really enjoyed the book because of its absurdly reductive philosophy that inadvertently plays on adolescent male narcissism like a jazz saxophone—to draw a connection to the famous Randian saxophonist and economist Alan Greenspan—but it also spoke directly to the adolescent male fantasy of "I'm the only smart one. Everyone is leeching off of me and I'd rather destroy my work than compromise my integrity by being nice to others." Her moral severity came as a tonic to my cultural relativist upbringing.

I started researching Rand and found that in her public appearances, she could be really funny, and purposefully so. I watched a couple of interviews that she gave to Phil Donahue between 1979 and 1981. By the time she was on Donahue, she knew that her life was coming to a close and therefore did not give a shit about anything anymore. She seemed to enjoy saying things that would make Donahue gasp, mostly about religion, God, and women, like that a woman shouldn't be president, which you knew she didn't believe. You could tell that Donahue loved her.

During one of those interviews, she revealed that her favorite television show was *Charlie's Angels*. Donahue was like, "Come on, Ayn Rand!" and she said, "It's a very good program. Why should I not enjoy it?" It's like, *just because I seem like a humorless scold, why should I not enjoy things that are enjoyable?* A show about three young, beautiful, talented women who were not accepted by the police department, and who, when forced into roles as traffic guards, became so incensed that they left to form a detective agency where they could shine—of course she loved *Charlie's Angels*! I began to think: What if Ayn Rand had written, in 1980, a weekly column for *Parade* about her favorite television shows? That was the backbone on which I based my impersonation for Tompkins. I would talk to him about the Village People and *Charlie's Angels* and why, because her moral philosophy is founded on the belief that there is an objective reality that man can perceive accurately, she can definitively and objectively say that the best movie of the year is *Caddyshack*.

I got this all planned, and then Paul called me and said, "Because we record this live in front of an audience, it's customary for the person impersonating the author to dress as the author." I told him that was fine and rented a dress from a costume shop in San Francisco—a frumpy, polyester, half business wear, half evening wear squared-shoulder dress that Ayn Rand would have worn in 1979 or 1980. It was the first time I had ever worn a dress (onstage or off). It was tremendously terrifying, especially since it was two sizes too small, but it was also liberating. I'd been wearing suits—and not just suits but three-piece suits—or tuxedos, things that were designed to protect and distract everyone from me. But now, as Rand, I was literally letting it hang out there, and it was transformative, maybe with a little emphasis on "trans," if you know what I mean.

I decided to continue performing as Ayn Rand in my stand-up act, or, rather, my standing up and

talking routine. I would make a request on Twitter ahead of time as I traveled around to do the act: if anyone had a dress, in a style that Rand might have worn that would fit a man of my proportions, and could bring it to the show, to let me know and I'd comp their ticket. It was very exciting to receive strange dresses and to change into them onstage, which I found a clever way to do by wearing a flesh-colored V-neck T-shirt and very dark colored underwear. Even though I was briefly near nude, I still felt protected as I slipped into the dress.

Then I reached Eugene, Oregon, and I don't know what it is about the people of Eugene—whether they don't own dresses in the style that Rand might have worn in 1979 or 1980, whether they guard them jealously, or whether they are just not a play-along kind of crowd—but despite my many entreaties, no one in the audience would come forward with a dress. As we drove into town and pulled into the strip mall where our hotel was located, John Roderick, with whom I was performing, saw a St. Vincent de Paul thrift store. "That's where you're going to get your Ayn Rand dress," he said. It was an amazing thrift store and indeed I found maybe half a dozen perfect dresses, all for under $50. I settled on a purple and electric blue number made entirely from man-made material with a very clever cross-broach fastener in the front, size eighteen. It was modest eveningwear for older ladies and big ladies, and it fit like a charm. I paid $20, put it on onstage, and became Ayn Rand.

Since then, I've performed in this dress a dozen times or more. This dress isn't different from any other Rand dress, except that it's mine. I own a dress, and it's the first dress that I have owned. From a theatrical point of view, it is perfect. It catches the light and shines a beacon of objective judgment across the entire crowd. It's indestructible. It does not wrinkle. You ball it up, throw it into a satchel, and bring it on the road, and it looks perfect the moment you take it out.

That brief moment of discomfort—that "what am I doing?" moment—and the transgression that I initially felt in San Francisco when I put on that dress for the first time is gone. Now, it's the part of the show that I look forward to the most. I no longer even wear that dumb flesh-colored T-shirt, although I still wear underwear because no one wants to see beyond that. But at a time when the work that I'm doing as a writer, as a performer, and as an actor is striving for less of the exaggerated gamesmanship of pretending to be an expert or deranged millionaire, and striving more to be authentically and vulnerably me, it is a real moment of power. For the audience, I think it's a powerfully disgusting moment—when I fully disrobe and stand for a period of time in only my underwear while trying to figure out if the dress is inside out or not before I put it on. Even though I'm imitating, in a ridiculous fashion, an exaggerated version of Ayn Rand, what precedes the moment of putting on the dress is an utter nudity of self, about as close as I'll ever get.

John Hodgman is an author, actor, and humorist, whose published works include *The Areas of My Expertise*, *More Information Than You Require*, and *That Is All*.

Heidi Julavits

This morning my eighteen-year-old neighbor came over wearing a sweater I'd owned in the eighties. It might have been my *exact* sweater—she found hers at a local thrift store for three dollars. Mine disappeared in a move a long time ago. This sweater, the L.L. Bean Norwegian Sweater, was once the most coveted item of clothing among the girls in my school. When too many people owned them, I started to wear mine inside out. The exposed yarn of the sweater's interior looked like crisscrossing electrical wires. I'm not sure if I pioneered this look or if I was copying somebody. I was probably copying one of the girls who attended the private school a few blocks from my house. I still remember the names of the girls who were not my friends, but whom I studied from a distance—Natasha, Rebecca, Joanna.

I not only studied what they wore, but also the wear patterns of their clothing. Wear patterns were what separated the naturals from the fakes. The naturals wore threadbare flannels with paint stains, patched jeans, faded and torn polo shirts, and sweaters with holes under the arms and at the cuffs. The most important wear detail to me, probably because I could never achieve it, involved the sneakers that the Natashas and the Rebeccas

and the Joannas wore. These sneakers were white canvas Tretorns. (Five years ago, a friend gave me a pair of Tretorns for my birthday. She meant the gift as a wink or a nod or a winky nod to the girls we'd both tried to be and never were.) When these girls wore their sneakers—and none of them would be caught dead with a new, white pair, which made me suspect that they wore them privately around their houses until they achieved the perfect scuffy patina—they looked like ballerinas. The toe of the sneaker came to a rounded point, the foot inside seemingly always arched. Most of them were not ballerinas, however, but tennis players, and thus the right front toe (if they were right-handed) often had a stringy puncture in it, and the front of the soles were worn down, because the girls dragged their right feet when they served.

I purchased the same sneakers but my feet did not wear them down correctly. The toes of my sneakers turned up and looked clownish. They did not look like ballet slippers, and they would never look like ballet slippers, no matter how many years I wore them. It was not a matter of commitment or self-confidence. These girls had something I could not purchase. Even when I was eleven I understood this.

Heidi Julavits is the author of four novels, including the PEN award–winning *The Vanishers*, the founding editor of *The Believer* magazine, a coeditor of *Women in Clothes*, and a professor at Columbia University.

Elisabeth Subrin

What does one wear for a breakup? In my periodic reassessment of the chunky, frayed, vintage sweaters I rarely wear anymore, there's one ragtag cowl-neck that's never been threatened with a Goodwill return. Not because its thin acrylic weave and form-fitting shape takes up less space in the drawer, nor because the horizontal, squiggly pattern might pass for Missoni in low light. I've always rationalized its stalwart place on my shelves because it looked good on me and *you never know...* plus it had potential use in one of my films. It could make a sexy, androgynous journalist look if paired with corduroy jeans, a blazer, and high-heeled vintage suede boots—think Maria Schneider in *All the President's Men.*

Despite the stretchy acrylic that reveals its birth in the Reagan years, the sweater nevertheless evokes my mother's seventies black turtlenecks, worn with silver link necklaces and bellbottom jeans. I probably found it while thrift shopping for films I made as a graduate student in Chicago in the nineties—a second layer of nostalgia. How I kept it relevant in millennial New York is a sartorial mystery. I was probably just holding out with my Riot-Grrrl-meets-*Network* look that had long been abandoned by the dotcom-infused scene (what was late-nineties fashion, anyway?). Now, mining subterranean associations, I found another reason I can't let it go.

Because what *does* one wear for a breakup? This is not a question I remember asking myself that frigid February night as I waited for him to come over for "the talk." But I have a vivid memory of pulling open those stiff, built-in drawers in my overheated railroad apartment and contemplating the shapely cowl neck of this sweater resting among odd late-nineties fibers. Breakups also come in many shapes and textures: "I'm breaking up with you and don't even consider breakup sex because I'm so over this" might call for very different outfit signifiers than "I'm breaking up with you but convince me not to," as opposed to "I'm breaking up with you because I suspect you might break up with me," and so on. In this case, it was somewhere between the second and third option, a preemptive strike with the irrational conviction that the outcome might nevertheless be different. My beloved sweater perfectly embodied that contradiction: The nonflirtatious flirt, the unsexy sexy. Covering up while revealing everything. Or, as he had described us: casual intensity.

The relationship had barely spanned two seasons, but I was in love with him and too scared to admit it. I couldn't believe that it would last because he was everything I desired at the time. I hid behind my film, a family crisis, a recent breakup, and a demanding job, grabbing at every defense I could find in order to avoid telling him how I felt. I was scared that my admission might push him away, when actually it was pushing me away. The sweater came off that night, but we never kissed again.

Elisabeth Subrin is a Brooklyn-based film and video artist and curator.

Rachel Comey

I'm about to open my first shop, which has been a long time coming. This past weekend, I walked by the storefront with my kids and took a picture of them in front of the empty space that will soon be my store. That photo reminded me of old photos of families proudly standing in front of their businesses, and it made me think about the legacy of the family business that I'm in the midst of creating.

Back in 2002 things were very different. I was living in a small apartment on the Lower East Side with my then-boyfriend Eugene, splitting the $400 per month rent. I was doing freelance work, doing anything anyone would hire me for. I'd stay out late absorbing young New York life. I was also making sets and costumes for Eugene's band, Gogol Bordello, and we were asked to be in the 2002 Whitney Biennial.

I remember a few things from the Biennial opening. It felt like a very big deal to go all the way uptown to the Whitney Museum. I wore a miniature hat, a flea market purchase that was kind of like a headpiece, because I thought it would be festive and appropriate. And Bill Cunningham took my picture. I didn't know who he was until the following Sunday when his photo of me in my little hat appeared in the *New York Times*.

Unfortunately, I can't find the newspaper clipping of me at the opening. I didn't save stuff like that. I was younger and it didn't really matter to me. Since then, not only am I more aware of preserving memories, I've also become a huge fan of Bill Cunningham. In fact, the first movie I took my newborn to was the Bill Cunningham documentary. It felt like a special occasion, and I documented the outing.

I learned that before Bill became a photographer, he'd been a hat designer. I like to think that had something to do with why he took my photo. I'd love to find the photo; one day, I'd like to tell my kids that story. For now, at least I still have the tiny hat.

—AS TOLD TO EMILY SPIVACK

Rachel Comey is a fashion designer living in New York.

Marcus Samuelsson

My mother and grandmother made most of my clothes when I was growing up. I'd ask for Levi's and my grandmother would say, "You want a pair of jeans? We can make that."

If you're American, it's hard to understand how aspirational America was for people like me, growing up in Ethiopia and then Sweden, particularly around brands like Converse, Levi's, Vans, and MTV. Especially when you're a thirteen-year-old kid wearing almost-Levi's that your mom made you with a raggedy Levi's tag sewn onto the pocket that she cut from somewhere else, along with brightly patterned hand-me-downs that were once worn by your sisters.

But the thing my mother and grandmother couldn't make was sneakers, and that made me want them even more.

By the time I got a scholarship to go to culinary school in Switzerland, I'd finally gotten my hands on a pair of Converse. Every day began with a daily lineup of all the chefs, and while most students wore Birkenstocks or Dr. Martens, I had on my slightly feminine turquoise Chuck Taylors. I wasn't supposed to wear them in the kitchen—nobody could enter the kitchen with sneakers—but if I was feeling rebellious, I wore my Converse. As a cook, you're taught that you aren't supposed to be seen, but that was impossible for me because as the only young black cook, I was seen the moment anyone entered the kitchen. So what did it matter if I wore Converse? The shoes were part of finding my identity as a person and as a chef.

Today I still wear my Converse, especially because of how versatile they are. I wear them in the kitchen when talking to the dishwasher, when I sit down for a meeting with my partners, and in the dining room of Red Rooster when it's showtime and I'm greeting the Knicks or Salman Rushdie or whoever comes through the restaurant that evening. When I get up in the morning, think about the day ahead of me, and know that I'm going to be on my feet constantly until I get home at midnight, no matter what else I'm wearing I want my Converse. I remember seeing this iconic picture of Mick Jagger mixing it up with his three-piece suit and pair of Converse and thinking, "That's how to own it."

—AS TOLD TO EMILY SPIVACK

Marcus Samuelsson is the Ethiopian-born, Swedish-raised chef and owner of Red Rooster Harlem and the author of *Yes, Chef*.

Sanya Kantarovsky

My great-grandfather on my mother's side was this legendary guy who was born in Crimea, fought in World War I *and* World War II, and served several years in prison for allegedly burning down a factory. He was respected by everyone for his ability to fight. He was a very little man who knocked out anyone he punched in the face.

He was given this belt when he fought in World War I, and he wore it fighting in World War II. He gave it to my grandpa, who then passed it along to me. It's a bit *Pulp Fiction*-y, although not exactly. One day, when I was about fifteen, I was at my grandparents' apartment and in need of a belt. My grandfather dug through his closet and found this dramatic-looking one, with its big Soviet star, and handed it to me. I wore it all the time.

I was wearing it the day I rented two scooters with three friends so we could drive to see a punk squat about an hour outside of Rome. We drove from the city's outer limits to the countryside, where we were surrounded by cornfields. The sun was beginning to set and my scooter started making these funny noises—it had run out of gas. We pulled over to a gas station in the middle of nowhere. I had never gotten gas in Italy before and was confronted with two pumps. One of them said *benzina* and one said *gasolio*. I'm Russian—in Russia, gasoline is *benzin* and in English it's *gasoline*. So in front of me was a Russian version and an English version of gasoline. I basically "eeny meeny miny moe-ed" it and filled the tank with *gasolio*.

Within a few hundred feet of the gas station, the scooter began making horrible gurgling noises. We pulled over to the side of the road, and a guy stopped behind us. We'd put diesel in the scooter,

he told us, and there was no way to get it out unless we had a siphon, which we didn't. We turned the scooter over in an attempt to pour out the diesel, but that didn't work. At this point, it was totally dark and the four of us were an hour away from Rome, so I did what I had to: I spent the next six hours shuttling everyone back to the city on the back of my scooter. Around three o'clock in the morning, I pulled up to my shivering friend Joe, who was sitting alone by a cornfield on the side of the road. He got on the scooter and we made the last trip back.

Because I spent so much time driving back and forth on the same route over the course of one night, several details remain very clear. I remember flying through red lights on the abandoned streets. I didn't feel like stopping since my friends were waiting for me. I remember initially concentrating on navigating through the unfamiliar streets, but by the third trip, I had memorized the route. It was a very strange experience, almost like *Groundhog Day*. It was springtime and I had on jeans, a sweater, a leather jacket from an old flea market in Rome, and my great-grandfather's belt.

I didn't consciously realize on that night—back when I was nineteen and wearing the belt because it looked cool—that its presence puts me at ease. It reminds me of home and of my family. Since I prefer less flashy belt buckles nowadays, I don't wear the belt anymore. But I throw it into my suitcase before every big trip, just to have it with me. It makes me feel more comfortable in whatever circumstance I find myself, like driving between Rome and some cornfields on a rented scooter six times in one night.

—AS TOLD TO EMILY SPIVACK

Sanya Kantarovsky is an artist living in Brooklyn.

Susan Bennett

When I moved to Atlanta, I was looking for professional opportunities related to music. I ended up doing a lot of jingle singing and backup vocals. A friend I'd worked with in the 1970s who lived in Nashville called and told me that Roy Orbison's backup soprano singer had been fired. They needed someone who could learn her parts quickly and who had a valid passport. "Any chance you're available for the gig?" my friend asked.

My very first gig with Roy was in 1982 at a music festival in Bulgaria that was televised to over ten million people. It was rather intimidating, but thrilling. While Roy wasn't in the limelight as he'd once been—in the 1960s The Beatles had opened for *him*!—he still had a sizable fan base around the world, especially in England and Australia. Shortly after the Bulgaria show, we went on a six-week tour in Australia. At the beginning of the trip, I bought a multicolored jacket with big shoulder pads, and it became my traveling jacket. For six weeks I wore a black jacket, black pants, and a sequined tube top onstage, but offstage I always wore this jacket.

Most of us rode around in a tour bus called "The Bitch." It was then that I could see why people got into trouble on tour—it's actually pretty boring unless you're somewhere that's exciting and you want to go sightseeing. Most people on tour didn't feel like going out. Since I wanted to see the local sites, I mostly hung out with the guitar and bass players who wanted to explore as well. Maybe it was because we were hanging around together that they wound up with jackets like mine—not identical, but a similar style with wacky colors. We got into the habit of referring to the jackets as our "Arnotts," like the Australian biscuit and snack company. Jimmy Johnson, the bassist, recently reminded me that when we wore the jackets, we'd pretend we were aliens. We had some alien words: *Arnott* was one, *Amso* was another, and although the famously reclusive Roy didn't have a jacket or participate, we dubbed him "Orbi 1 Con Orbi."

Touring with Roy came to an end after an adventurous two years. I only wish, though, I'd left *after* Roy's performance on *Saturday Night Live*.

—AS TOLD TO EMILY SPIVACK

Susan Bennett is a singer and voice-over artist who is most widely known for being the voice of the original U.S. version of Apple's Siri.

Pamela Jones

It was a floral dress, midlength, with pearl buttons down the front. Because it was the early to midnineties, it had big shoulder pads. I paired it with dyed black satin stilettos with scalloped edges and pointy toes that I thought were the sexiest shoes.

I was an accounting manager for a trucking company (where I still work after thirty-three years) that hauled produce. One of our offices is in the two hundred–person town where I live, Big Cabin, Oklahoma. We're country people, and we wear jeans to work. Six of my colleagues and I had been invited to a very nice dinner at an annual produce convention and trade show in Montreal, which was a big deal. It wasn't formal, but it was dressy. Because none of us had anything appropriate to wear, the company's owner had taken us shopping in Tulsa, about an hour away.

On the evening of the dinner, it had been snowing, so we shared two cabs. One cab pulled up pretty far from the curb. To get into the backseat, and to save my beautiful heels from the slush on the road, I had to step across the curb and place my feet on the doorframe. Instead, my feet slid, catapulting me across the backseat. I found myself face down with my feet hanging out the door. Can you imagine?

I gathered myself up and saw that three of my colleagues were laughing. I could tell that all my makeup had rubbed off on the car seat, including my filled-in eyebrows! I started laughing, too. Once we settled into the cab, still in hysterics, I realized that the little *ping! ping!* sounds I'd heard when I slipped had come from a couple of buttons popping off my dress. One flew into the front seat and one was in the backseat, leaving holes in my dress. We hadn't even left and I'd already ruined my outfit!

When we arrived at the dinner, a red carpet led to the door of the venue. It felt like there was a

hole I kept stepping into as I limped on that carpet. I asked a colleague, "What's wrong with this carpet?" "Nothing!" she responded, confused. Indeed the carpet was not full of holes. Rather, when I had fallen into the cab, I had knocked the heel off one of my shoes, and I was hobbling along with one heel!

We headed to the bathroom so that I could straighten up. I tried to fix my shoe's heel but the entire sole was coming off. I was laughing so hard that tears were running down my face. I reached up to wipe off the mascara streaks and a colleague yelled, "Don't touch your face!" I'd forgotten my shoes were dyed and, because they were wet, the dye had turned my hands black.

The company owners, who had taken the other cab, arrived and found us in hysterics. They were upset because they thought we'd been drinking and partying and acting a fool, and they wanted us to behave ourselves. Once we told them what had happened, though, they were sympathetic.

We decided that I'd just sit in a chair and everyone would do their socializing, we'd eat and leave, and nobody would be the wiser. But when I stepped into the ballroom, the host ran up to me and said, "Oh my goodness! Are you okay?" The owners of the company had told him the story before we got upstairs, so suddenly everyone was paying attention to the girl with the ripped dress, no heel, no makeup, no hose, and black hands.

As it turns out, the meal was really good. I sat still. I drank a lot of wine because one of the waiters kept refilling my glass. I was definitely wobbling on one heel when we returned to the hotel that evening. As soon as I got back to my room, I threw my heels in the trash and never looked back. But I couldn't part with the dress, even if my daughter thinks it's the ugliest thing she's ever seen.

—AS TOLD TO EMILY SPIVACK

Pamela Jones is a manager for a produce-trucking company in Big Cabin, Oklahoma.

Karuna Scheinfeld

My dad has a uniform that he's been wearing for the past twenty years. When he was younger, he was more experimental, like when my parents got married he wore a purple suede cowboy suit. Now, though, he only wears a blue oxford shirt, gray flat-front Brooks Brothers wool trousers, black socks, and a white undershirt. So if we went canoeing, that's what he'd be wearing. If he went to a business meeting, that's what he'd be wearing. If he went to a wedding, that's what he'd be wearing. If he went to the beach, that's what he'd be wearing, but with swim trunks instead of pants. It's become endearing. My family will tease him—this little Jewish man and his uniform.

Around 2003 I was helping him organize his closet. In its depths, I came upon one of his forty or so oxford shirts. It was from the eighties and it had that classic preppy look I was into. A more slender cut, a softer fabric, and it fit me well. Most significantly, it had his initials, *D. R. S.*, monogrammed on the pocket, which I was immediately drawn to.

But it was that monogram that actually turned him off and got the shirt relegated to the back of his closet. My father's brother Jim had given him the shirt thinking the monogram was a nice detail, but to my father, it represented "the man." My father's father was a businessman, and his brother was a businessman, and he had rejected that path to become an anthropologist.

As his daughter, though, I loved the idea of wearing a shirt with his initials.

He gave it to me and I started wearing it all the time—to the point that I got a little psycho about it. I was wearing the shirt every week. I would bring it to work to show them how I wanted the shirts I was designing to feel—but I would never let them keep it. I started acting really paranoid. I traveled for work a lot and would wear it on every trip, but I wouldn't pack it in my checked luggage. I would wear it on the airplane—to China, Peru, India. I knew I was being ridiculous, but then my luggage got stolen and that confirmed it. I realized there was no way to *not* wear it on every flight. Who knew what could happen to it!

Even though my father is healthy, he's eighty-one and has entered old age, so his death is on my mind. During my four years living in Italy, so far apart from my parents in Chicago, that kind of anxiety gave the shirt more weight.

Over time I wore the oxford so much that it began to fall apart, to fray and tear. I'd repair it, but when one of the sleeves ripped off, it reached a point where I felt like I couldn't wear it anymore.

I had a friend named Guy who was a painter in Tel Aviv. He'd been doing a series of paintings of everyday objects, so I commissioned him to make a painting of the shirt. I wanted it to act as a memorial—I just couldn't bear to let it go.

When he was working on it, I'd get emails like, "Karuna, this shirt, it's killing me. So simple and yet so complicated!" He's appropriately dramatic. He wound up making two paintings of it. Both are abstract, distilling the shirt to its essential elements, but each is slightly different. He gave me one and I bought the other—I didn't like the idea of anyone owning them but me. Now one hangs in my office and the other in my bedroom.

—AS TOLD TO EMILY SPIVACK

Karuna Scheinfeld is the vice president of design at Woolrich and lives in Brooklyn.

Sherry Turkle

My purple sweatshirt, well, it's not quite a sweatshirt at all. It is a cotton waffle weave. It has little holes where mice ate away at it. But that is why I love it.

I bought it as one of my comfy mommy outfits, when my husband and I adopted our daughter Rebecca. I never really was much for sweatpants and soft shirts, but a baby seemed to call for this new garb since the baby wore such soft things. I was thin and stylish; it was the early 1990s, and all of my clothes seemed rough to the touch when I was around the baby. I wanted fleece.

From the moment I held Rebecca in my arms I loved her wonderful baby body. How she smelled, the light blue vein on the bridge of her nose, the smell of powder on the top of her head. I made up rituals around changing diapers and bath time. At diaper time I would say "Creeeam," as I dabbed on the diaper ointment. "Creeeam," she would laugh back. At bedtime, we counted her baby blankets as I tucked her in. Pink Blankie, White Blankie, Flannel Blankie, Waffle Weave Blankie. At eight months Rebecca put Waffle Weave Blankie against my purple sweatshirt and pointed from one to the other. It led to a song: "Waffle weave. Yellow. Purple. Becca. Mommy."

Most of all, I loved feeding Rebecca. Since I had not been able to nurse her, giving her a bottle, having her body that close, was precious to me. When she was born, MIT, where I taught, had no parental leave for mothers who had adopted children. (Childbirth counted as "medical leave." Adoption counted for nothing.) I worked full time when Rebecca was an infant. I missed so much time with her, so many bottles. I still get upset thinking about this.

When Rebecca was one, I took a leave of absence. I needed to be closer to my child, and my husband and I were having problems. We moved from the city to the country. We dreamed that this would help: a life in the country with our new baby, a lack of city pressures, waking up to the possibilities of our beautiful garden. But now it was winter. We couldn't see possibilities.

One night I was giving Rebecca a bottle after her bath, and before I had a chance to burp her over my shoulder, protected by a cloth diaper, she spit up all over the front of my purple sweatshirt. The macaroni and cheese of that evening's dinner had not agreed with her. I grabbed a few baby wipes. I wiped my shirt. I wiped her soft mouth and changed her pajamas. I sang my daughter to sleep as I always did with the lullabies of my childhood: "Tura Lura Lura," the theme song from *The Goldbergs* television hour, and "You Are My Sunshine."

Getting ready for bed, I took the purple shirt off and threw it on the hamper. I looked around the big house for my husband. He waved me away; he was watching television in his study.

That night, mice feasted. When I saw the holes in the morning, the spit-up of macaroni and cheese eaten away, I washed the shirt carefully and put it back on. Soft, with its traces of Rebecca—Rebecca was where the shirt was not—it comforted me. It still does. Perverse? It's possible. I'm wearing the purple sweatshirt now, twenty-one years later, and it still reminds me of the season when I had my life's sweetest and saddest moments at the same time. I was closest to my baby's body and frozen out by the winter that was supposed to bring me back to the man I loved.

Sherry Turkle is the Abby Rockefeller Mauzé professor of the social studies of science and technology at the Massachusetts Institute of Technology, and the author of numerous books, most recently, *Alone Together: Why We Expect More from Technology and Less from Each Other.*

Becky Stark

I was heartbroken, disoriented, devastated. My life felt torn in a way that was scary. I had been so bonded to him that with him gone and our bond broken, I was gone, too. Shamans say that when people get sick, they're experiencing soul loss. That's what I had. Soul loss. And I didn't know what to do to regain my soul.

My mother claims that I didn't speak until I was nearly four years old and then suddenly I began speaking in complete sentences. My first was, "Why are you dressing me like a boy?" I wanted to wear dresses, and not short dresses, but long dresses.

I have always derived great pleasure from dressing up. I'm fairly easily delighted, and dressing up is the easiest pathway to delight for me. It's a way of thinking of every day as a holiday.

In my life, I have dress fairies, dress angels. I never buy anything new. I mostly shop the dollar rack at thrift stores, and I always find what I need. I cycle through dresses and then sell them back to thrift stores. I don't need to hold on to them.

But during the time when I was experiencing soul loss, I was wearing weird, ill-fitting jeans and a gray shirt. I had no joy in anything, especially when it came to dressing up.

My friend Shara was in Los Angeles to perform in an opera. She came to visit me when I was in my half-life state and basically wearing rags. "Why don't we go to the little dress shop around the corner?" she asked me. Normally, I would love to go to a dress shop, but I didn't want to go. "I want to buy you a present for your birthday," she justified, as my birthday was approaching.

I conceded, and we went to the shop. But none of the dresses were beautiful to me—it was the weirdest feeling. Shara kept trying to ignite some flame of life in me.

"How about this one?" she'd ask.

"I woulda used to like that one," I'd respond.

"How about this one?"

"I woulda used to like that one…"

Nothing. Shara was persistent.

"We have to keep looking!"

If we found something, I knew she didn't have the money to buy me a $150 dress. And even if a dress had cost one dollar, I couldn't have bought it either. "They're all too expensive," I told her. She was determined. "It doesn't matter. Keep looking."

Amid a rack with dresses from the forties, one dress caught my eye—and it was actually beautiful to me! It was heavy crepe, teal, and floor-length.

"Why don't you try it on?" Shara asked.

"It's going to be too expensive." I just knew.

"Then why don't you see how much it costs?"

When I found the price tag, *free* was written on it. It had to be a mistake; the dress was too beautiful.

I took it to the woman at the counter. "Excuse me. Why does this dress say that it's free?"

"Because it's free. I have so many dresses, and the hem needs to be fixed. I thought it might make someone happy, and it's for you."

I started crying. I said, "Thank. You. So. Much."

I call it a dress miracle. I didn't even try it on at the shop. I waited until I got home. When I slipped it on, it fit me like a glove, like it was made for me.

I know the shop owner was just thinking she'd do something nice for someone. But she really helped me. This dress healed my heartache. It brought my soul back to me. Some burdens you can't lift by yourself, but someone else, from another vantage point, can help. I know it's just a dress. I know the woman at the shop just saw a little tear and decided to make it free; it didn't appear out of thin air. Rationally, I understand all of those things. But this stranger's simple act of generosity lifted me out of my sorrow, making me once again love the dresses that I woulda used to love.

—AS TOLD TO EMILY SPIVACK

Becky Stark is an artist, singer, songwriter, and the voice of the band Lavender Diamond.

ACKNOWLEDGMENTS

Worn Stories is the result of many people's generosity. First, to all the contributors to the book and to the website: thank you for your time and for your stories.

This book would not have been possible without the tireless enthusiasm, indispensable input, and unwavering dedication of Giselle La Pompe-Moore, who helped manage this project, and for that, I am deeply grateful. Moreover, I am thankful to Alessandro Esculapio for his ongoing assistance, commitment, and quick wit.

I am especially appreciative of my agent, Jud Laghi, for believing in this concept early on, and Jennifer Lippert, Meredith Baber, and Paul Wagner at Princeton Architectural Press for their vision and contributions. For her keen eye and ability to bring everything I could have hoped for to the book's photography, thank you to Ally Lindsay.

I'm indebted to my family—Marcy Spivack, Dennis Spivack, and Lauren Spivack—for their steadfast support, and for not being afraid to tell me what they really think.

A handful of people have been invaluable sources of support, encouragement, good ideas, and solid advice, in particular Catherine Pierce, Amanda Katz, Joshuah Bearman, Stacey Reiss, Michael Bell-Smith, and Shana Lutker.

Many thanks, as well, to Meredith Barnett, Laura Davis, Jelani Day, Roberta Golinkoff, Jessamyn Hatcher, Laura Jane Kenny, Lystra La Pompe, Hanne Mugaas, Danica Newell, Maria Popova, James Ryang, Tal Schori, Josh Siegel, Larry Smith, Jen Snow, Emily Ziff, and the countless people who made introductions and suggestions, and who spread the word along the way.

To the woman who strolled into Philadelphia's Institute of Contemporary Art to attend my first ever *Worn Stories* workshop many years ago, and unzipped her puffy winter coat to reveal a green satin ball gown whose story she'd been waiting to tell, thank you for confirming my hunch.

Published by
Princeton Architectural Press
37 East Seventh Street
New York, New York 10003

Visit our website at www.papress.com
Visit *Worn Stories* at www.wornstories.com

The Louise Bourgeois text on page 5 was reprinted with permission from
Louise Bourgeois, *The Return of the Repressed, Volume II: Psychoanalytic Writings*
(London: Violette Editions, 2012), 144.
Louise Bourgeois, c. 1968. Loose sheet: 11 × 8 ½ in. (27.9 × 21.6 cm); LB-0202.
© The Easton Foundation.

The photograph on page 92: Marina Abramović on the Great Wall of China, 1988.
Courtesy of the Marina Abramović Archives.

A version of Davy Rothbart's story appears in his collection of personal essays,
My Heart is an Idiot (New York: Farrar, Straus, and Giroux, 2012).

Editor: Meredith Baber
Designer: Paul Wagner
Photography: Ally Lindsay

Special thanks to: Sara Bader, Nicola Bednarek Brower, Janet Behning, Megan Carey,
Carina Cha, Andrea Chlad, Barbara Darko, Benjamin English, Russell Fernandez,
Will Foster, Jan Haux, Diane Levinson, Jennifer Lippert, Katharine Myers, Jaime Nelson,
Jay Sacher, Rob Shaeffer, Sara Stemen, Marielle Suba, and Joseph Weston
of Princeton Architectural Press —Kevin C. Lippert, publisher

Library of Congress Cataloging-in-Publication Data is available from
the publisher upon request.